Marcel Kielhorn

The Constitution for Europe

EUROPA 2000

Studien zur interdisziplinären Deutschland- und Europaforschung

herausgegeben von der

Arbeitsstelle für Interdisziplinäre Deutschland- und Europaforschung am Institut für Politikwissenschaft der Westfälischen Wilhelms-Universität Münster

Prof. em. Dr. Karl Hahn, Prof. Dr. Peter Nitschke, Martina Husemann-Lüking, Kerstin Kellermann, Georg Breuer, Karsten Roesler, Philipp Hermeier

Band 22

LIT

Marcel Kielhorn

The Constitution for Europe

The Point of no Return?

LIT

Bibliographic information published by Die Deutsche Bibliothek
Die Deutsche Bibliothek lists this publication in the Deutsche
Nationalbibliografie; detailed bibliographic data are available in the
Internet at http://dnb.ddb.de.

ISBN 3-8258-8756-1
Zugl.: Aberdeen, Univ., Diss., 2004

A catalogue record for this book is available from the British library

© LIT VERLAG Münster 2005
Grevener Str./Fresnostr. 2   48159 Münster
Tel. 0251-62 03 20   Fax 0251-23 19 72
e-Mail: lit@lit-verlag.de   http://www.lit-verlag.de

Distributed in North America by:

Transaction Publishers
New Brunswick (U.S.A.) and London (U.K.)

Transaction Publishers
Rutgers University
35 Berrue Circle
Piscataway, NJ 08854

Tel.: (732) 445-2280
Fax: (732) 445-3138
for orders (U. S. only):
toll free (888) 999-6778

For my parents, grandparents and Sandra

The unity of Europe was the dream of few, it has become the hope for many and today it is the necessity for all.

(Dr. Konrad Adenauer, Government Statement FRG 15 December 1954)

TABLE OF CONTENTS

Table of Contents

TABLE OF CONTENTS	**VIII**
PREFACE	**2**
ABSTRACT	**4**
INTRODUCTION	**7**

PART I
Legal Possibility and Practical Necessity of the EU-Constitution — **12**

1.	The Term "Constitution"	12
1.1.	The "classic" Definition	13
1.2.	Appropriateness of the "classic" Definition for the EU	13
1.2.1.	The New Concept	14
1.2.2.	The *demos* Question	15
1.3.	A (Constitutional) Treaty as a Constitution: Legal Possibility ?	19
1.3.1.	No more than a Treaty	20
1.3.2.	A Treaty as Constitution	20
1.3.3.	Evaluation and Conclusion	22
1.4.	Intermediate Conclusion	23
2.	Does Europe already have a Constitution ?	24
2.1.	The Legal Framework of the EU	24
2.2.	Constitutionalization of the Treaties by the ECJ	25
2.2.1.	Doctrines and the Court's Language	25
2.2.2.	Consequence	27
2.3.	International Treaties or de facto Constitution ?	29
2.4.	Intermediate Conclusion	32
3.	Necessity of a (formal) Constitution	32

3.1.	Declarations of Nice and Laeken in 2001	33
3.2.	Influence of the Enlargement	34
3.3.	Symbolic Value	35
3.4.	Intermediate Conclusion	36
4.	The Myths concerning the European Constitution	37
4.1.	The Creation of a Super-State	37
4.2.	European Constitution swallows National Constitutions	38
4.3.	Extensive EU-Powers over Foreign Affairs, Defence and Employment Laws	39
5.	Intermediate Conclusion to Part I	39

PART II
A Successful Advance on the Treaty System ?   42

1.	Advantages and Disadvantages of written Constitutions	42
2.	Determination and Assessment of Success	43
3.	Declarations of Nice and Laeken	43
4.	Simplification and Reorganization of the Treaties	44
4.1.	Meaning of Simplification and Reorganization	44
4.2.	One Union	45
4.3.	The (unfinished) Merger of the Pillars	46
5.	Analysis of specific Parts of the Constitutional Treaty	47
5.1.	The Union of the People	47
5.2.	The "Exit-Clause"	48
5.3.	Fundamental Principles, Rights and Values	49
5.4.	Decision-Making in the (European) Council	51
5.5.	Competences and Powers	53
5.5.1.	The Competences	53
5.5.2.	The Principle of Subsidiarity	54
5.5.3.	The Flexibility Clause	55
5.5.4.	Intermediate Conclusion	56
5.6.	The new Institutional Order	57
5.6.1.	Increasing Democratic Legitimacy and Transparency	58
5.6.2.	Improving Efficiency	59

5.7.	Simplification of Legal Instruments..................................	61
6.	Intermediate Conclusion...	63

PART III
Brussels 2004: Effects, Aftermath and Referenda 65

1.	Finally an Agreement...	65
2.	Strengthened or Weakened – the Effects of the Agreement...	67
3.	The Aftermath OR The Problem of Ratification	68
3.1.	Provisions in the European and National Constitutions..	68
3.2.	Consequences of Non-Ratification	68
3.2.1.	Retry..	69
3.2.2.	Exclusion of "Naysayers"..	69
3.2.3.	Two-speed Europe	70
3.2.4.	Majority decisive..	70
3.2.5.	A European Referendum	71
3.3.	Intermediate Conclusion...	73

PART IV
Concluding Remarks 75

APPENDICES
Appendix 1	79
Appendix 2	83
Appendix 3	85
Appendix 4	88
Appendix 5	99

BIBLIOGRAPHY 104

PREFACE

PREFACE

Many important changes have occured during the 16 years since the collapse of the 'iron curtain' which divided Europe in its heart in 1989: The first stage of the EMU came into effect in 1992, the declaration of Laeken called for substantial changes concerning the structure of the institutions and the law in 2001, the Euro became the official and sole currency for twelve Member States in 2002 and the number of Member States rose to 25 by the enlargement in 2004. Further, the Treaty establishing a Constitution for Europe was agreed on and signed the same year and Spain was the first country to hold a referendum in February 2005.

With the Constitutional Treaty being ready for ratification the EU is at the crossroads: Either it will take a further step towards a closer than ever continent realizing and benefitting from its political, economic and cultural power or it might suffer a heavy setback by denying ratification which could possibly ruin the 50-year old vision of a free, prosperous and united Europe.

This work was submitted as LL.M.-thesis at the University of Aberdeen (U.K.) in September 2004. It has been revised and now reflects the *status quo* of April 2005. The monography shall contribute to the ongoing discussion on the necessity, qualities and effects of the Constitutional Treaty. However, this book cannot provide an in-depth account of all sections of the document but it can analyse, emphasize and visualize the importance of a common Constitution for Europe.

My thanks go to the library staff of the University of Aberdeen and especially to my supervisor and teacher Ms Carole Lyons who guaranteed the success of my work due to her continuous support, critique and feed-back.

Cologne, April 2005   Marcel Kielhorn

ABSTRACT

ABSTRACT

On 19 June 2004 the 25 Member States of the European Union agreed on a provisional version of the Constitutional Treaty which was signed on 29 October 2004 in Rome. Three Member States have already ratified the document and Spain was the first country to hold a referendum. The objective of this dissertation is to argue that as a result of these events the European Union is soon to be, from a legal point of view, at a point of no return.

This dissertation starts with the examination of the legal possibility and practical necessity of a constitutional future of the EU. It develops an EU appropriate definition of the term "constitution" by modifying the traditional view of the *demos* question. It further scrutinizes the necessity of a formal Constitutional Treaty in the light of the declarations of Nice and Laeken, the influence of the recent enlargement and the symbolic value of constitutions. The thesis also exposes three myths concerning the Constitutional Treaty.

The second part discusses whether the Constitutional Treaty could be said to be a successful advance on the current Treaty system. In the light of the goals set out in the Declarations of Nice and Laeken it analyses specific parts of the Constitutional Treaty in this respect.

The final part scrutinizes the way an agreement was finally reached at the IGC in Brussels 2004 and its (worldwide) effects. Moreover, the much disputed issue of ratification is dealt with: the new legal provisions are discussed, possible consequences of non-ratification by one or some Member States are explored and the possibility of a European-wide referendum, is considered.

INTRODUCTION

INTRODUCTION

At the late hours of 19 June 2004 the Representatives of the Governments of the 25 Member States of the European Union (EU) finally agreed on a (provisional) version of the draft Treaty establishing a Constitution for Europe.[1] Within Europes history of more than 50 years[2] this certainly was one of the most difficult, fiercely discussed and controversial hurdles the Union had to clear.

25 different countries influenced the future basic legal text of the EU for 25 different political, cultural or historical backgrounds, 21 different recognized languages, 450 million people. A document prepared to support "the peoples of Europe [...] to transcend their ancient divisions and, united ever more closely, to forge a common destiny".[3]

These are great visions and boundless ambitions – but is the Constitution, and with it the whole EU, capable of fulfilling them ? If so, the Constitution without a doubt would be the point of no return for an ever closer union among the peoples of Europe and their countries.[4]
But what is the real deal ? Will the EU be better off with the (new) Constitution ? Does it really need one ? Does it not already have one ? Can it have one at all ? Will it ever enter into force ?

---

[1] CIG 87/04 *Treaty establishing a Constitution for Europe*; Referred to throughout, for ease, simply as "the Constitution", "EU-Constitution" or "Constitutional Treaty".
[2] See Appendix 1, "The History of the EU".
[3] Preamble of the Constitutional Treaty (CT).
[4] Cf. Preamble of Part II of the Constitutional Treaty.

Is it a "dense legal text, with simplicity sacrificed on the altar of political compromise" ?[5] Were "the leaders of the Union [...] determined to strengthen the ship on which the Europeans have set sail [and ...] did so by adopting the first European Constitution" ? Or did they (and consequently the Constitution) present the sorry sight of a mutinous crew, unable to agree on the name of the captain, squabbling over whose hand should be on the tiller, and with no idea which direction to head" ?[6] Or is it simply a "historic step forward in the process of integration and cooperation of Europe [... with a] Constitution [establishing] an efficient, democratic and transparent framework for the future development of the Union" ?[7]

As these citations indicate, opinions about the Constitution are diverse. After 52 years, the Union stands at the crossroads,[8] entering into a transitional period which will determine the EU's fate.

To answer the questions raised above is the objective of this thesis or, in other words, this thesis attempts to explain why the Constitution ought and has to be ratified and how that might be best done.

---

[5] G. Parker in the *Financial Times*, as cited by K. Chhor, *Western Press Review*, http://www.truthnews.com/month/2004060100.htm; see Appendix 4, "Press Reviews".

[6] Both Editorial in *Liberation*, as cited by BBC news "Press relief over EU deal", http://www.news.bbc.co.uk/1/hi/world/europe/3821533.stm, on Web July 2004.

[7] 10679/04 ADD 1, *Addendum to the Cover Note of the Presidency Conclusions of the Brussels European Council 17 and 18 June 2004*.

[8] *Laeken Declaration* (15/12/2001), http://europa.eu.int/futurum/documents/offtext/doc151201_en.htm.

Part I examines the legal possibility and practical necessity of a European Constitution. In order to obtain a satisfactory result the term "constitution" itself is determined according to the classic definition. As this definition was elaborated for national constitutions it does not seem to be appropriate to the EU, so that a new concept with a revised *demos* thesis is presented, which even accepts constitutions to adopt the form of a treaty. Further, that chapter deals with the question whether the EU does not already have a constitution. Recognizing the existence of a functional constitution the next section shows why a formal constitution nevertheless is a necessity – and mere amendments of the existing Treaties would not be sufficient. Additionally, two myths from the eurosceptic camp are exposed: The creation of a European super-state via the Constitution and the end of national constitutions.

Thereafter, Part II focuses on the question whether the Constitutional Treaty is an advance on the current Treaty system and has to be seen as a success. Only if both parts of that question can be answered in the affirmative, a ratification would be recommendable and a wise decision – otherwise, the *status quo* could be kept and political energy be invested in other projects of the EU. Firstly, the decisive parameters for the determination and assessment of success are established: The fulfilment of the objectives set out in the Declarations of Nice and Laeken:[9] (i) Enhancement of democratic legitimacy, transparency and effectiveness, (ii) new allocation and delimitation of powers and com-

---

[9] *Nice Treaty Declaration No 23* (26/02/2001): Declaration on the Future of the Union, http://europa.eu.int/eur-lex/en/treaties/dat/nice/html; *Laeken Declaration*.

petences, (iii) simplification and reorganization of the Treaties and (iv) the inclusion of the Charter of Fundamental Rights. Secondly, the EU-Constitution is scrutinized in the light of these objectives by an analysis of the new structure as a whole and additionally by looking at several specific parts of the Constitutional Treaty.

Lastly, Part III evaluates the IGC of Brussels 2004, trying to answer why an agreement finally had been reached although just six months earlier the vision of a European Constitution already seemed to be on its deathbed. Also, the possible effect of the outcome and the previous constitutional process is assessed in terms of having strengthened or rather weakened the EU. This chapter is concluded by a close look at the problematic aftermath of the summit: The ratification of the Constitution. The process is explained and potential scenarios are discussed for the (likely) case of one ore more Member States encountering difficulties with ratification.

Will the EU soon arrive at the point of no return ? This dissertation attempts to show how, why and possibly when we are getting closer to this point.

PART I

LEGAL POSSIBILITY AND PRACTICAL NECESSITY OF THE EU-CONSTITUTION

PART I

Legal Possibility and Practical Necessity of the EU-Constitution

"Neither morals, nor riches, nor discipline of armies, nor all these together will do without a constitution."
(John Adams)[10]

Why does the EU, why do we need the recently agreed Constitution ? Does the EU not already have one ? If so, what makes it still a necessity ? These is the first bundle of questions which has to be tackled in order to deliver a supportive answer to the aforementioned thesis. Otherwise, i.e. if the necessity-argument had to be dismissed, there would be no need for a ratification of the Constitutional Treaty.

1. The Term "Constitution"

First of all, as the term "constitution" is not as self-evident as it might be supposed, the common comprehension of the term will be explained. Subsequently, it will be examined whether the elaborated definition is appropiate for a legal, economic and political entity such as the EU.

---

[10] John Adams (1735-1826), 2nd President of the United States of America (1797-1801) as quoted by S. Douglas-Scott, *Constitutional Law of the European Union* (2002), p. 515.

1.1. The "classic" Definition

An undisputed feature of constitutions is that they are primarily concerned with political authority and power.[11] According to the traditional view a constitution contains, *inter alia*, rules and practices that determine the composition and functions of the organs of government in a state, the exercise of sovereign powers, regulate the rights of individuals and their protection.[12] In their entirety, constitutions are considered as the fundamenal law of a nation or state epressing a common ideology.[13] Many scholars even conclude that States alone may have constitutions[14] because the legitimacy of a constitutional text requires a pre-existing sovereign state entity based on a pre-existing social substrate.[15]

1.2. Appropriateness of the "classic" Definition for the EU

As it becomes obvious from the aforementioned definition, the traditional concept of constitution was established and developed at a time

---

[11] S. de Smith and R. Brazier, *Constitutional and Administrative Law* (8th ed., 1990), p 6; B. Thompson, *Textbook on Constitutional and Administrative Law* (3rd ed., 1998), p 4.

[12] According to the definition in B. A. Garner, *Black's Law Dictionary* (7th ed., 1999), p 306; E. A. Martin, *A Dictionary of Law* (4th ed, 1997), p 99; J. E. Penner, *Mozley and Whiteley's Law Dictionary* (12th ed., 2001), p 72.

[13] De Smith and Brazier, *op. cit.* n 11, p 4; J.-C. Piris, "Does the European Union have a Constitution? Does it need one?", (1999) *24 E.L.Rev.* 557-585 at p 558; J. Raz, "On the Authority and Interpretation of Constitutions: Some Preliminaries", in L. Alexander (ed.) *Constitutionalism: Philosophical foundations* (1998), pp 153 f.

[14] J. Isensee, "Staat und Verfassung", in J. Isensee and P. Kirchhof (eds), *Handbuch des Staatsrechts Bd. 1* (1987), § 13 notes 1-8.

[15] K. Lenaerts and D. Gerard, "The structure of the Union according to the Constitution for Europe", (2004) *29 E.L.Rev.* 289-322 at p 293.

when national states and their constitutions emerged.[16] Thus, this concept cannot be taken over without being questioned with regard to the developments within the EU which consists of 25 sovereign Member States.[17]

1.2.1. The New Concept

In a Union of 25 Member States the classic state-centred view has lost ground giving way to the prevailing view of an more "abstract" or "post-national" concept of constitution.[18] According to that even documents containing rules for the operation of an organization might be called constitution.[19] This concept rather focuses on the contents than on the origin, i.e. national state or organization, of a document. For the assessment of the Constitutional Treaty

> it is essential to see that the instrument by which the European level of government is created and sovereignty is pooled has the same function as a national constitution: it establishes institutions, provides them with limited competencies and powers, or-

---

[16] USA (1787), France (1789), German Empire (1871) amongst others.

[17] J. Dutheil de la Rochère and I. Pernice, "European Union Law and National Constitutions", in M. Andenas and J. A. Usher (eds), *The Treaty of Nice and Beyond: Enlargement and Constitutional Reform* (2003), 47-105 at p 54.

[18] Dutheil de la Rochère / Pernice, *op. cit.* n 17, p 54; M. Nettesheim, "EU-Recht und nationales Verfassungsrecht: Deutscher Bericht", in Lord Slynn of Hadley and M. Andenas (eds), *FIDE XX. Congress London 2002, Volume 1, National Reports* (London: British Institute of International and Comparative Law, 2002), 81 at p 90 f; I. Pernice, "Die neue Verfassung der Europäischen Union – ein historischer Fortschritt zu einem Europäischen Bundesstaat ?", (2003) *FCE Spezial 1/03 Speech at the Urania Berlin*, 1-23 at p 4; N. Walker, "Postnational Constitutionalism and the Problem of Translation", (2003) *Working Paper IILJ 2003/03*, 1-36 at p 30 f.

[19] Thompson, *op. cit.* n 11, p 3.

ganises the political process, [...] and defines the status and rights of the individual as a citizen of this community."[20]

Consequently, the Constitutional Treaty of the EU is not *a priori* incapable of being considered as a constitutional order.

1.2.2. The *demos* Question

Eurosceptics state that a European Constitution would lack legitimacy and Europe was not even able to have one as there does not exist an alleged necessary prerequisite: A European people, a European *demos*. The EU would lack a sufficient degree of homogeneity.[21] According to the *Bundesverfassungsgericht* "[e]ach of the peoples of the individual States is the starting point for a state power relating to that people".[22] Constitutions could only be realised in the national framework and a theoretical possible (but unlikely) European *demos* would automatically replace the national *demoi*.[23]

This assertion does not get to the crucial point and is arguable in certain aspects: The key question is not whether there is a single Euro-

---

[20] Dutheil de la Rochère / Pernice, *op. cit.* n 17, p 55 f.; also see N. Walker, "European Constitutionalism and European Integration", (1996) *Public Law* 266-290 at p 270: he sees the need for a functional rather than a formal view of constitutions.
[21] Cf. N. Walker, "Constitutionalising Enlargement, Enlarging Constitutionalism", (2003) *9 E.L.Rev.* 365-385 at p 373: "The EU [...] lacks [...] the relatively thick cultural identity of the national [...] state" and further "the strong cultural ties of a common language, traditions, history, affective symbols, and developed civil society and public sphere".
[22] *Brunner v The European Union Treaty* [1994], 1 C.M.L.Rev. 57 at para. 44.
[23] D. Grimm, "Does Europe need a Constitution ?", (1995) *1 E.L.J.* 282-302 at p 297.

pean *demos* but rather whether the existing *demoi* are acting on several levels, i.e. on national plus European level and thus may nevertheless enable and legitimize a European Constitution.

The outdated idea of unity of nationality and citizenship has to be given up in favour of a decoupled concept. The reason is that, especially in the Member States of the EU, people do no longer regard themselves as merely being a national and citizen of a certain state but rather feel, at least to some degree, as Europeans, too.[24] Moreover, through the denationalisation of capital investment, culture, travel and communications media, the classic state of the Westphalian age has come to an end.[25] Furthermore, a new concept opens the possibility of thinking of co-existing multiple *demoi* which concentrate on civic and political rather than on ethno-cultural terms.[26] This idea is strongly supported by the preambles respectively of the Treaty of Rome[27], the Treaty on European Union (TEU)[28] and most recently of the Constitutional Treaty[29]. These preambles have in common that they all see a European people

---

[24] See Appendix 2 "National vs European Identity".
[25] N. Walker, "The Idea of Constitutional Pluralism", (2002) 65 *M.L.Rev.* 317-359 at p 320.
[26] J. H. H. Weiler, "Does Europe Need a Constitution ? Demos, Telos and the German Maastricht Decision", (1995) *1 E.L.J.* 219-258 at pp 240 ff.; J. H. H. Weiler, *The constitution of Europe: 'Do the new clothes have an emperor?' and other essays on European integration*, (1999) p 344.
[27] "Determined to lay the foundations of an ever closer union among the peoples of Europe [...]".
[28] "[...] deepen solidarity between their peoples while respecting their history, their culture and their traditions [...]"; "[...] to establish a citizenship common to nationals of their countries [...]"; "[...] reinforcing the European identity [...]".
[29] "[...] Convinced that, while remaining proud of their own national identities and history, the peoples of Europe are determined to transcend their ancient divi-

both as the starting point and as the *terminus* of the European integration process. The European identity [which exists in form of a common cultural heritage, i.e. a cultural and political identity[30]] is the presupposition of the process of integration [...] [and t]his shared identity, this single European demos, by no means precludes the existence of a plurality of diverse European peoples on which it is based: there is unity in diversity.[31]

The European concept of *demos* is different from the nationality-based citizenship but nevertheless constitutes a *demos* of its own.[32] Consequently, it can arguably be stated that there are yet multiple and complementary *demoi* in Europe.[33]

Moreover, it does not become obvious why it should be impossible for a legal norm to produce a legal entity ?[34] The same sort of argument was put forward when the European Monitary Union (EMU) was created: According to the basic economic rules a monetary union requires a pre-existing and functioning political union with its own economic and financial policy.[35] Despite ignoring these textbook rules the EMU turned out to be a success – or to put it in other words: "The question of the necessary identity pre-existing any legitimate constitution is the

---

sions and, united ever more closely, to forge a common destiny, [...] Convinced that, thus "united in diversity" [...].

[30] A. Peters "European Democracy after the 2003 Convention", (2004) *41 C.M.L.Rev.* 37-85 at p 75 f.

[31] M. Brand, "Affirming and Refining European Constitutionalism: Towards the Establishment of the First Constitution for the European Union", (2004) *EUI Working Paper LAW No. 2004/2*, 1-58 at p 11.

[32] Weiler, *op. cit.* n 26, p 344.

[33] See Appendix 2, "National v European Identity".

[34] Brand, (2004) *EUI Working Paper LAW No. 2004/2*, p 10.

[35] R. Leicht "Mission Impossible: Verfassung für Europa", http://zeus.zeit.de/text/archiv/2002/10/200210_verfassgsmodelle.xml, para 8.

typical 'chicken and egg' dilemma, as to who has to come first."[36] Hence, there is no reason why a "reversed" and unorthodox approach should not be applied again – this time to the constitution.

Another aspect which by some analysts is considered as an huge obstacle to the evolution and creation of a common identity is the absence of a European *lingua franca*, a common language to all Europeans. However, this theory exaggerates the importance of language amongst the diverse factors contributing to identity-formation.[37] Despite being true that a common language simplifies the communication and as a consequence identity-building[38] there are multiple examples where states are comprised of several nations with different languages but nevertheless build a homogeneious entity.[39] This clearly proves that states and constitutions may also be based on a plurality of nations and languages.[40]

On the account of the abovementioned it becomes obvious that there is no need and no justification for a pre-existing people or single Euro-

---

[36] Lenaerts / Gerard, (2004) *29 E.L.Rev.*, p 295.
[37] E. J. Hobsbawm, *Nations and Nationalism since 1780* (1990), pp 20-22; 54-63; 97-100.
[38] J. Habermas, "Why Europe needs a Constitution", (2001) http://www.newleftreview.net/NLR24501.shtml, 1-16 at p 8.
[39] Switzerland with its Italian-, German- and French-speaking parts, India with more than 20 languages or South Africa; F. Mancini, "Europe:The Case for Statehood", (1998) *4 E.L.J.* 29-42 at p 29; Pernice, (2003) *FCE Spezial 1/03 Speech at the Urania Berlin*, pp 7 f; for opposite opinion see J. H. H. Weiler, "Europe: The Case Against the Case for Statehood", (1998) *4 E.L.J.* 43-62 at p 59.
[40] Brand, (2004) *EUI Working Paper LAW No. 2004/2*, p 15.

pean *demos*.⁴¹ Since the notion of "constitution" is older than the one of "state" or the one of the modern "demos" the latter simply cannot be a prerequisite.⁴² Moreover, it is possible to have several *demoi* within one entity which means that European and national identities, the civic *demos*, is not competitive but complementary, cooperative and co-existent.⁴³ This view is confirmed by an opinion poll conducted in the 25 Member States in spring 2004.⁴⁴ According to that survey, the majority of citizens detected some European element in their national identity. Thus, a common European cultural heritage in some way exists and with it a European *demos*.⁴⁵

Consequently, the European Union in my view is capable of having a constitution.

1.3. A (Constitutional) Treaty as a Constitution: Legal Possibility?

On 18 June 2004, the representatives of the governments of the Member States agreed on a Constitutional Treaty. But what does that mean? Is it legally possible to have a constitution in form of a treaty? These

---

[41] Habermas, (2001) http://www.newleftreview.net/NLR24501.shtml, p 8; Peters, (2004) *41 C.M.L.Rev.*, p 71.

[42] Even international organizations have constitutions; C. Dorau / P. Jacobi, "The Debate over a 'European Constitution': Is it Solely a German Concern?", (2000) *6 E.P.L.* 413-428 at pp 417 f.

[43] Cf. Brand, (2004) *EUI Working Paper LAW No. 2004/2*, p 17; U. Di Fabio, "The European Constitutional Treaty: An Analysis", (2004) *5 G.L.J.* para 15, http://www.germanlawjournal.com, on Web August 2004; Peters, (2004) *41 C.M.L.Rev.*, p 76; Walker, (2002) *65 M.L.Rev.*, p 351; Weiler, (1995) *1 E.L.J.*, pp 254 ff.

[44] Eurobarometer, "2004 Spring – Comparative Highlight Report", p 23; see also Appendix 2.

[45] M. Brand, (2004) *EUI Working Paper LAW No. 2004/2*, p 17; Peters, (2004) *41 C.M.L.Rev.*, pp 75 f.

questions will be dealt with in the following only as the question about the nature of the current treaties and the EU will be discussed later on.

By calling the legal document a "Constitutional Treaty" the emphasis may either be put on the term "constitution" or on the term "treaty".[46]

1.3.1. No more than a Treaty

The arguments highlighting the treaty-aspect are as follows:

The document was agreed upon as a treaty between sovereign states and future amendments will be conducted in the same manner.[47] Further, it contains Protocols and Declarations typical for common treaties. Moreover, the title clearly states that the Constitutional Treaty is merely another treaty. Therefore, the legal paper does not have the status of higher law which is a common feature of traditional constitutions.[48] Thus, from a strictly legal point of view the Constitutional Treaty is a treaty which replaces the preceding treaties of the EU.[49]

1.3.2. A Treaty as Constitution

Opposing to this position it is submitted that it is not enough to look at the formal aspects only but also attention has to be paid to the larger picture, i.e. the symbolic and political value of the Constitutional

---

[46] P. Eleftheriadis, "Constitution or Treaty ?", (2004) *Online Paper 12/04* http://www.fedtrust.co.uk, 1-12 at p 3, on Web August 2004.
[47] Art. IV-436 CT.
[48] Cf. Eleftheriadis, *op. cit.* n 46, p 4.
[49] K. Hänsch, "Der Verfassungsentwurf für die Europäische Union nach der Regierungskonferenz", (2004) *Forum Constitutionis Europae FCE 2/04 Speech at the Humboldt-University Berlin*, 2-8 at 7; cf. also Art. IV-2 DT.

Treaty.[50] In the light of that argument the Constitutional Treaty represents a crucial step in the process of an "ever closer union" by its effort to make the EU more transparent, understandable and "runable".[51]

> Historisch ist sie [der Verfassungsvertrag] nichts weniger als die Neugründung der Europäischen Union [...] [da s]ie Europa eine neue Ordnung und eine neue Perspektive geben [muss].[52]

The establishment of the Constitutional Treaty via the convention-method further promotes the character of a constitution because the fundamental law of the EU is directly (via the Convent) and indirectly (via the Governments / Member States) legitimized by the exercise of public power so that its designation as "constitution" appears adequate.[53] The merger of the Treaties is a major constitutional step for the EU, but even more so is the insertion of the Charter of Fundamental Rights[54], the expression of values common to "the peoples of Europe"[55] and the new allocation of competences[56]. Accordingly, although the

---

[50] J. Kokott / A. Rüth, "The European Convention and its Draft Treaty establishing a Constitution fo Europe: Appropriate Answers to the Laeken Questions ?", (2003) 40 C.M.L.Rev. 1315-1345 at p 1320.
[51] Hänsch, FCE 2/04 Speech at the Humboldt-University Berlin, p 7; Kokott / Rüth, (2003) 40 C.M.L:Rev. p 1321.
[52] Hänsch, FCE 2/04 Speech at the Humboldt-University Berlin, p 7: "Historically, it [the Constitutional Treaty] is no less than the re-foundation of the European Union [... as i]t [must] give Europe a new order and a new perspective." (translation by the author).
[53] S. Hobe, "Bedingungen, Verfahren und Chancen europäischer Verfassungsgebung", (2003) 38 Europarecht, 1-16 at pp 6 f, Kokott / Rüth, (2003) 40 C.M.L.Rev. p 1320; Lenaerts / Gerard, (2004) 29 E.L.Rev., p 298.
[54] Part II Arts II-61 to II-114 CT.
[55] Part I Titles I-II, Preamble Part II CT.

Constitution takes the form of a treaty [it] does not affect its constitutional nature [...]. In addition, the Convention has marked a switch of perspective, from a formal constitution enacted through substantive treaty-making, to a substantive constitution the adoption of which is operated [...] by formal treaty-making.[57]

1.3.3. Evaluation and Conclusion

The aformentioned makes obvious that the European Union and its fundamental legal text, the Constitutional Treaty, cannot simply be interpreted as a constitution in the common sense by solely assessing its contents, though it certainly possesses constitutional features. It has to be ackknowledged that the Governments on behalf of their respective Member States retain decisive influence, for instance via the ratification and amendment procedure. It is true that such procedures are not unknown to foreign (national) constitutions[58] but the EU and its Constitutional Treaty cannot be compared to national constitutions as the former serves a different aim, tries to unite while still respecting diversity and different identities from 25 Member States with its own historical backgrounds.[59] As a supranational agreement between States

---

[56] Part I Title III Arts I-11 to I-18 CT.
[57] Lenaerts / Gerard, (2004) *29 E.L.Rev.*, p 298.
[58] Lenaerts / Gerard, (2004), *29 E.L.Rev.*, p 298; Art. V US Constitution: "The Congress, whenever two-thirds of both houses shall deem it necessary, shall propose amendements to this Constitution, or, on the application of the legislature of two-thirds of the several states, shall call a convention for proposing amendments, which, in either case, shall be valid to all intents and purposes, as part of this Constitution, when ratified by the legislatures of three-fourths of the several states, or by conventions in three-fourths thereof, as the one or the other mode of ratification may be proposed by the Congress; [...]".
[59] M. Dzurinda, "The Debate on the European Constitution – A Slovak View", (2002) *FCE Spezial 1/02 Speech at the Humboldt-University Berlin*, 2-8 at p 4;

the Constitutional Treaty has legally to be considered as a treaty but in the political and historical context it is at the same time a constitutional document for the grounds given before.

The facts given one should begin to perceive the EU as new constitutional order between national states, legitimized not by just a single but by a double basis: the citizens and the Member States.[60] Conventional legal theories and analogies to state law should be abandoned and the Constitutional Treaty should be seen as the springboard for a constitutional theory that recognizes the Union's unique nature, "its position between constitutional and international law".[61] The Constitutional Treaty is a new step in constitutional law and theory – it is a *sui generis* Constitution based on a "neo-constitutional" theory adjusted to contemporary constitutional needs for the unique entity of the EU.

1.4. Intermediate Conclusion

According to this new definition of the term "constitution" the EU may (i) have a constitution which (ii) even may be concluded in the form of a treaty.

Hänsch, *FCE 2/04 Speech at the Humboldt-University Berlin*, p 7; Pernice, (2003) *FCE Spezial 1/03 Speech at the Urania Berlin*, p 3.
[60] Dutheil de la Rochère / Pernice, *op. cit.* n 17, p 58.
[61] Eleftheriadis, *op. cit.* n 46, pp 4 f., 11.

2. Does Europe already have a Constitution ?

In order to assess the necessity of a European Constitution it is indispensable to settle the question whether the EU does not already have a constitution. If the answer is in the affirmative stronger arguments supporting the necessity of a "new" constitution will have to be provided.

2.1. The Legal Framework of the EU

The EU with its three-pillar structure[62], which was established by the Treaty of Maastricht (1992), is currently governed by several treaties: The Treaty establishing the European Community (1957), the Treaty establishing the Atomic Energy Community (1957) and the aforementioned Treaty establishing the European Union (1992).[63] The Treaty establishing the European Coal and Steel Community (1951) expired in 2002.[64] The Treaties were concluded as traditional multilateral agreements between the Governments of the Member States.[65]

---

[62] The three pillars are: The Community pillar (corresponding to the three Community treaties, cf. TEC), the Common Foreign and Security (CFSP) pillar (Art. 11-28 TEU) and the justice and home affairs (JHA) pillar (Art. 29-45 TEU).

[63] The founding treaties have been amended several times by (i) the Merger Treaty (1965), (ii) the Single European Act (1986), (iii) the Treaty of Amsterdam (1997) and (iv) the Treaty of Nice (2001). From six Member States at the very beginning in 1951 the EU has grown to 25 Members States in 2004; also see Appendix 1 "The History of the European Union".

[64] M. Piepenschneider, "Vertragsgrundlagen und Entscheidungsverfahren", (2003) *279 Informationen zur politischen Bildung*, 17-26 at p 17; O. Schmuck, "Reformperspektiven und Verfassungsfragen", (2003) *279 Informationen zur politischen Bildung*, 53-59 at p 58.

[65] Lenaerts / Gerard, (2004) *29 E.L.Rev.* 289-322 at p 297; K. Lenaerts / M. Desomer, "New Models of Constitution-Making in Europe: The Quest for legitimacy", (2002) *39 C.M.L.Rev.* 1217-1253 at p 1221.

2.2. Constitutionalization of the Treaties by the ECJ

Although the initial nature of the Treaties as international treaties negotiated under international law which gave birth to an international organization[66] it is submitted that the Court of Justice constitutionalized the Treaties.

2.2.1. Doctrines and the Court's Language

It has done so through its so-called "fundamental jurisprudence", i.e. especially via its doctrines of direct effect[67], supremacy[68] and state-liability[69], which have been accepted by Member States' governments, national courts and authorities.[70] The ECJ confirmed and further developed the doctrine of direct effect in several cases including *Defrenne*[71] and *van Duyn*[72] (for directives). The doctrine of supremacy was consistently further developed in the later cases of *Internationale*

---

[66] Weiler, *op. cit.* n 26, p 221.
[67] Case 26/62 *NV Algemene Transport – en Expeditie Onderneming van Gend en Loos v Nederlandse Administratie der Belastingen* [1963] ECR 1.
[68] Case 6/64 *Flaminio Costa v Ente Nazionale per l'Energia Elletrica (ENEL)* [1964] ECR 585.
[69] Joined Cases C-6/90 & C-9/90 *Andrea Francovich and Others v Italian Republic* [1991] ECR I-5357; The following criteria had been fulfilled: The Directive involved rights on individuals which contents could be indentified by the provisions of the Directive and there was a causal link between the State's failure and the damage suffered by the the persons affected.
[70] Brand, (2004) *EUI Working Paper LAW No. 2004/2*, p 19; S. Weatherill, "Is constitutional finality feasible or desirable? On the cases for European constitutionalism and a European Constitution", (2002) *Constitutionalism Web-Papers, ConWEB No. 7/2002*, URL http://les1.man.ac.uk/conweb/, on Web July 2004
[71] Case 149/77, *Defrenne v SABENA* [1979] ECR 1365.
[72] Case 41/74 *van Duyn v Home Office* [1974] ECR 1337.

Handelsgesellschaft[73], *Simmenthal*[74] and *Factortame*[75] as the so-called keystone of the doctrine of European constitutionality.[76] The scope of the doctrine of state-liability was extended by *Factortame No. 3*[77] and most recently by *Köbler*[78]. Of similar constitutional effect are the doctrines of implied powers, pre-emption and the Court's jurisprudence on fundamental rights.[79]

But not merely the doctrines itself deserve the merits for contributing to the alleged constitutionalization of the Treaties but to an equivalent extent does the use of specific "Community-descriptive" terms by the ECJ:

In *van Gend en Loos* the Court held that the EC Treaty constitutes a new legal order of international law.[80]

---

[73] Case 11/70, *Internationale Handelsgesellschaft mbH v Einfuhr- und Vorratsstelle für Getreide* [1970] ECR 1125.

[74] Case 106/77, *Amministrazione delle Finanze dello Stato v Simmenthal SpA* [1978] ECR 629.

[75] Case C-213/89, *Factortame Ltd v Secretary of State for Transport (No. 2)* [1990] ECR I-2243.

[76] Douglas-Scott, *op. cit.* n 10, p 260.

[77] Joined Cases C 46 and C-48/93, *Brasserie du Pêcheur v Germany* and *The Queen v Secretary of State, ex parte Factortame* [1996] ECR I-1029: Provided that the *Francovich* conditions are fulfilled, Member States are liable for breaches of all Community law whether or not directly effective.

[78] Case 224/01, *Gerhard Köbler v Republik Österreich*, judgment of the Court of 30 September 2003, para. 50: The principle is also applicable where the alleged infringement stems from a decision of a court adjudicating at last instance.

[79] Brand, (2004) *EUI Working Paper LAW No. 2004/2*, pp 19 f.

[80] Case 26/62, *van Gend en Loos* [1963] ECR 1 at 12 f: "The objective of the EEC Treaty [...] implies that this Treaty is more than an agreement [...] between the contracting states [...] the Community constitutes **a new legal order of international law** for the benefit of which the states have limited their sovereign rights

Just a year later the ECJ stated in *Costa v ENEL* that

> [b]y **contrast with ordinary international treaties**, the EEC Treaty has created its own legal system which [...] became an integral part of the legal systems of the Member States and which their courts are bound to apply.[81]

22 years on, the Court eventually made clear in *Les Verts* that the Treaty was the basic constitutional charter of the Community.[82]

2.2.2. Consequence

Accordingly, the ECJ established the primacy of Community Law "over any conflicting national rules and policies and helped to transform these provisions from elements of an intergovernmental agreement into the core of an [at least] economic constitution".[83] Consequently, it may be asserted that the principles of direct effect, supremacy and state liability formed the centrepiece of the EC's legal order. The Court of Justice has, as indicated previously, consistently devel-

---

[...] and the subjects of which comprise not only Member States but also their nationals."; emphasis added by the author.

[81] Case 6/64, *Costa v ENEL* [1964] ECR 585 at 593; emphasis added by the author.

[82] Case 294/83 *Parti écologiste 'Les Verts' v European Parliament* [1986] ECR 1339 at p 1365: "The European Economic Community is a Community based on the rule of law, inasmuch as neither its Member States nor its institutions can avoid a review of the question whether the measures adopted by them are in conformity with the **basic constitutional charter, the Treaty**."; emphasis added by the author; see also *Opinion 1/91* [1991] ECR I-6079 at p I-6080; Case C-314/91 *Beate Weber v European Parliament* [1993] ECR I-1093 at p I-1109.

[83] G. de Búrca, "The constitutional challenge of new governance in the European Union", (2003) *28 E.L.Rev.* 814-839 at p 817.

oped these principles.[84] The ECJ has done so by widening the scope of the doctrine's application[85], and it has specified certain criteria which have to be met before a principle applies in different areas of Community law[86] or by confirming its former judgments in subsequent cases.[87] The fact, that Community law was radically changed, shaped and influenced through these decisions plus the constant recognition of these principles within the Member States justifies the conclusion that the judgments had a fundamental impact on Community law and constitutionalised the Treaties.[88] Making international norms directly applicable and endow them with a higher status has to be acknowledged as constitutionalization or bestowal of constitutional status to the respective norm.[89]

---

[84] Piris, (1999) *24 E.L.Rev.* 560.

[85] See development from *van Gend en Loos* via *Defrenne* to *van Duyn* or development from *Francovich* to *Köbler*.

[86] E.g. conditions for direct effect of provisions of the Treaty and different conditions for Directives.

[87] An outstanding example is the principle of supremacy which reoccurs in many cases subsequent to *Costa v ENEL*.

[88] G. A. Bermann, "Editorial: The European Union as a Constitutional Experiment", (2004) *10 E.L.J.* 363-370 at p 365; F. Mancini, "The Making of a Constitution for Europe", (1989) *26 C.M.L.Rev.* 595-614 at p 595; It is true that the fundamental jurisprudence of the ECJ has been criticized harshly as allegedly being "excesses of judicial law making" and "judicial activism" but this does not withstand the abovementioned final assessment of the constitutionalization of the Treaties. This is so as judicial creativity is inevitable and remains inside the lawful scope of judiciary functions or, as Sir D. Edwards put it on p 65 of his article "Judicial Activism – Myth or Reality ? *Van Gend en Loos, Costa v ENEL* and the *Van Duyn* family revisited", it was and still is the Court's obligation to ensure the observation of the law, i.e. the interpretation as well as the application of Community Law.

[89] Cf. J. H. Jackson, "Status of Treaties in Domestic Legal Systems: A Policy Analysis", (1992) *86 American Law Journal of International Law* 310-340 at p 330.

2.3. International Treaties or de facto Constitution?

Despite the fact that the Court constitutionalised the Treaties to some extent the status of the Treaties as a whole requires further disucussion.

As the Treaties were signed as multilateral intergovernmental agreements it may be argued, from a purely formalistic point of view, that such a treaty will always remain a treaty regardless any effects or provisions resembling those of a constitution.[90] According to critics, Community law is merely a sub-system of international law.[91] The unusual characteristics of the Community Treaties do not, as in the opinion of the sceptical analysts, justify the believe that the founding fathers intended to provide the Community with a legal order of its own.[92] The different unusual features could even be found in other international treaties.[93] According to that point of view any decisions of the ECJ in regards to direct effect, supremacy or any other substantial area of Community law cannot alter the very nature of the original founding document of the EC.

This perception of the Treaties of the EC is questionable for several reasons: The EC was shaped as a unique form of an international organization with, for such an organization, unusual law-making, juris-

---

[90] Maduro, *We the Court: The European Court of Justice and the European Economic Constitution* (1997), p 8.
[91] T. Hartley, *The Foundations of European Community Law: An Introduction to the constitutional and administrative law of the European Community* (5th ed, 2003), p 89.
[92] Hartley, *ibid.*, p 135 f.
[93] Hartley, *ibid.*, p 132 f.

prudential and institutional powers.[94] The Treaties already contain elements in the constitutional sense, e.g. provisions about the composition and function of its organs (Art. 189 ff. EC) including provisions about law-making powers, important rights for the citizens of the EU (*inter alia* Art. 12, 17 ff. EC), the rule of law (Art. 6 TEU) or (qualified) majority voting.[95] Moreover, the power to legislate directly applicable law in the form of decisions, regulations and (if the implementation was flawed) directives also has to be considered as constitutional competence.[96] These facts clearly show the peculiarity of the Community and its law already. However, the most important contribution was made by the previously mentioned fundamental jurisprudence of the ECJ. These principles are said to have transformed the original Treaties to a new constitutional legal order.[97] It is true that especially the doctrines of direct effect and supremacy were key elements in the process of transformation. After they were proclaimed by the Court the Treaties more and more became an unprecedent new legal order. However, the argument, that therefore EC law has been constitutionalised

---

[94] Mancini, (1989) 26 *C.M.L.Rev.*, p 595.

[95] Other fundamental values to be found in the Treaties are: principles of openness, closeness to the citizens and solidarity among Member States and their peoples (Art. 1 TEU); principle of sustainable development (Art. 2 TEU); elimination of inequalities and the promotion of equality between men and women (Arts 3 (2) and 141 EC); principle of subsidiarity (Art. 5 EC); the protection of the environment (Art. 6 EC), the prohibition of discrimination based on sex, racial or ethnic origin, religion or belief, disability, age or sexual orientation (Art. 13 EC).

[96] Piris, (1999) 24 *E.L.Rev.* 561.

[97] Case 26/62, *van Gend en Loos* [1963] ECR 1 at 12; Case 6/64 *Costa v ENEL* [1964] ECR 585 at 593; Case 294/83 *'Les Verts'* [1986] ECR 1339 at p 1365; Pollicino, (2003) 5 *G.L.J.* 284, *et al.*

> acquired an element of circularity [...] At first, supremacy and direct effect were to be recognized because the EC Treaty was unlike other international treaties [...] [b]ut now that these principles have been accepted everywhere [...] the direction of the argument is often reversed: EC law is now often presented as being unique because it is endowed with direct effect and supremacy.[98]

Nevertheless, since the original EC Treaty with Art. 177 already empowered the ECJ to interpret EC law, it is "commonplace for courts to read into treaties or constitutions provisions that are not found explicitly therein".[99] Thus, the new doctrines have to be accepted as fundamental Community law which transformed the original Treaties into a new legal order. The argument that the founding fathers of the Treaties may not have intended the development EC law from a mere multilateral treaty towards a new (constitutional) legal order as it happened via the case-law of the Court of Justice without having an express provision inserted into the Treaty[100] cannot be upheld since there is no obvious proof for or against this hypothesis in the Treaties. Further evidence for the opinion that

> even if the EEC did conform to the status of an international organisation in its early days [...] it has now moved well beyond that [...] may be found in the fact that EU treaties may not be amended according to the rules of international law.[101]

---

[98] B. de Witte, "Direct Effect, Supremacy, and the Nature of the Legal Order", in P. Craig and G. de Búrca (eds), *The Evolution of EU law* (1999), 177-213 at p 208.

[99] P. Craig, "Constitutions, Constitutionalism and the European Union", (2001) 7 *E.L.J.* 125-150 at p 131.

[100] Hartley, *Constitutional Problems of the European Union* (1999), p 25.

[101] Douglas-Scott, *op. cit.* n. 10, p 260.

2.4. Intermediate Conclusion

Consequently, the Treaty possesses superior legal value which clearly meets the most important elements defining a constitution.[102] However, this does not necessarily signify that the initial multilateral international treaty has been transformed into a constitutional order. The Treaties may merely be seen as a constitution in the functional sense, i.e. a constitution-in-practice or "de facto" constitution, but not as one in the formal sense.[103]

3. Necessity of a (formal) Constitution

As the EU has already an implicit constitution it is inevitable to ask for the reasons which still make it necessary to adopt a constitution. In other words, it has to be examined why it would not be enough to introduce the reforms by the traditional method, i.e. Treaty amendments via the Intergovernmental Conference (IGC).[104]

---

[102] Craig, (2001) 7 *E.L.J.* 129; Piris, (1999) 24 *E.L.Rev.* 559, 561. Penner, *op. cit.* n 12, p 133.

[103] Brand, (2004) *EUI Working Paper LAW No. 2004/2*, p 42; Dutheil de la Rochère / Pernice, *op. cit.* n 17, p 56; N. MacCormick, *A Union of its Own Kind ? Reflections on the European Convention and the Proposed Constitution of the European Union* (2004), pp 19 f.

[104] Cf. Di Fabio, (2004) 5 *G.L.J.* at para. 10; Dzurinda, (2002) *Forum Constitutionis Europae FCE Spezial 1/02 Speech at the Humboldt-University Berlin*, p 4; N. Walker, "The EU as a Constitutional Project", (2004) http://www.fedtrust.co.uk/default.esp?pageid=1878&mpageid=67&msubid=75&groupid=6, 1-10 at p 4.

3.1. Declarations of Nice and Laeken in 2001[105]

Both documents deal with the future role of the EU and necessary changes in order to play a major part in a globalized world. The main concerns are the (re-)allocation of powers, the status of the Charter of Fundamental Rights of the EU, a simplification of the Treaties and the achievement of a clearer, more open, more effective and more democratic and democratically legitimized political Union. The adoption of a constitutional text was just a vague long-term objective.[106] The simplification was meant to be reached without changing the contents of the current Treaties.

The "re-foundation of the Union's legitimacy" was thought to be produced through a democratic process involving a Convention resembling those creating a constitution.[107]

Nice and Laeken paved the way for a democratic constitutionalization of the Treaties but did not see a Constitution for Europe as a necessity. However, as there is no better way to gain democratic legitimacy than by the support of its citizens for a common Constitution the legitimacy-argument strongly supports the view that a constitution is a necessity.[108]

---

[105] *Nice Treaty Declaration No 23* Declaration on the Future of the Union; *Laeken Declaration*.

[106] *Laeken Declaration*, Chapter II subheading "Towards a Constitution for European citizens".

[107] Lenaerts / Gerard, (2004) 29 E.L.Rev. 321.

[108] Cf. Douglas-Scott, *op. cit.* n 10, p 522; Lenaerts / Gerard, (2004) 29 E.L.Rev. 321; Thym, "European Constitutional Theory and the Post-Nice Process", in M. Andenas and J. A. Usher (eds), *The Treaty of Nice and Beyond: Enlargement and Constitutional Reform* (2003), 147-180 at p 153.

3.2. Influence of the Enlargement

Another factor which might render a European Constitution a necessity is the latest enlargement of the EU from 15 to 25 Member States and likely future enlargements to 27 or even 28 in 2007.[109] Despite the opinion of the Heads of Governments of the Member States at the end of the IGC in Nice that "the way for enlargement of the European Union [is opened ... and] the European Union [has] completed the institutional changes necessary for the accession of new Member States"[110] many institutional questions remained unanswered: The smooth running of a Union of 25 States was not ensured and the Treaty remained silent on the question how to the democratic legitimacy of the institutions could be obtained.

The decision-making procedure and democratic legitimacy had to be improved in order to get the EU ready for the 2004 Enlargement. The traditional approach via a "bargaining" IGC failed as became clear by the conference of Nice in 2001.[111] Thus, the idea to employ a proposal-preparing convention proved to be the most sensible alternative. However, this solely supports another manner of preparations of the IGC, i.e a change of the institutional design, and Treaty amendments but does not feed the necessity-argument.

---

[109] Current Member States since 01/05/2004: Austria, Belgium, Cyprus, Czech Republic, Denmark, Estonia, Finland, France, Germany, Greece, Hungary, Italy, Ireland, Latvia, Lithunia, Luxembourg, Malta, Netherlands, Poland, Portugal, Slovakia, Slovenia, Spain, Sweden, UK – possible future Member States are: Bulgaria, Romania, Turkey.

[110] *Nice Treaty Declaration No 23*, para 2.

[111] Schmuck, (2003) *279 Informationen zur politischen Bildung* 54; E. Teufel, "Konturen der Europäischen Verfassung", (2003) *FCE 3/03 Speech at the Humboldt-University Berlin*, 1-12 at p 1.

3.3. Symbolic Value

Often underrated but certainly the strongest argument in favour of a neccesity for a European Constitution is the symbolic value and the effects of constitutionalism especially on legitimacy: It mobilises the Community and may contribute to a polity affirmation.[112]

An EU-Constitution would first of all affirm the fact that the EU (and former EC) has developed, as has always been claimed by the ECJ, from an international, economic entity into a constitutional entity with its own legal personality.[113] It would bring the process of integration on its final route and include many elements achieved during the EU's constitutionalization process which started back in 1963 with the judgment in *van Gend en Loos*.

Further, the symbolic significance of the incorporation of the Charter of Fundamental Rights into a document bearing the word "Constitution(al)" cannot be overestimated as it resembles the guarantees given by national constitutions to its citizens.[114]

Moreover, constitutions have a limited but certain community-strengthening potential, capable of creating and nourishing a European constitutional awareness enabling the peoples of Europe to perceive themselves as belonging to a common European polity.[115] The constitutional consciousness will certainly, as it has to some extent already

---

[112] Walker, (2003) *9 E.L.Rev.* 369.
[113] Brand, (2004) *EUI Working Paper LAW No. 2004/2*, p 44.
[114] Cf. Thym, *op. cit.* n 108, p 165.
[115] Cf. Brand, (2004) *EUI Working Paper LAW No. 2004/2*, p 44; Douglas-Scott, *op. cit.* n 10, p 523; Thym, *op. cit.* n 108, p 165.

done during the drafting period of the Constitutional Treaty, encourage public discussion and participation and hence "boost the legitimacy of the Union".[116]

The Constitution, as a symbol of consensus on shared values and integration, would be an important identity-building measure which would strengthen the European political community by capturing the hearts and minds of Europeans and might even facilitate the development of a (thicker) European *demos*.[117]

3.4. Intermediate Conclusion

According to the previously mentioned findings only a Constitution or Constitutional Treaty would have effects which enhanced transparency and legitimacy to a remarkable extent. Also fostering a European identity could not be mastered better than by the adoption of a Constitution. It is true, that in some areas amendments of the Treaties could be sufficient but to make a further step in the European integration transition, to create a common spirit among Europe's citizens and as an expression of European unity the Constitution is a necessity.[118] Also,

---

[116] Douglas-Scott, *op. cit.* n 10, p 522; Lenaerts / Desomer, (2002) *39 C.M.L.Rev.* 1234.

[117] Cf. Dutheil de la Rochère / Pernice, *op. cit.* n 17, p 48; R. Goring, "Requirements for the Emerging European Constitution", (2003) *WHI-Paper 2/03 Humboldt-University Berlin*, 2-15 at p 10; Hänsch, *FCE 2/04 Speech at the Humboldt-University Berlin*, p 7; Lenaerts / Gerard, (2004) *29 E.L.Rev.*, p 322; Thym, *op. cit.* n 108, p 166; Walker, (2003) *9 E.L.Rev.* 370; Cf. the situation of the EU to the constitutional settlements in the renewal of the states and societies of Central and Eastern Europe after the fall of Soviet Communism or the post-apartheid era of South Africa from 1995 (see Walker, (2004) http://www.fedtrust.co.uk/default.esp?pageid=1878&mpageid=67&msubid=75&groupid=6, p 5).

[118] Dzurinda, *FCE Spezial 1/02 Speech at the Humboldt-University Berlin*, p 4.

without a constitutional frame and the "natural" authority of a constitution the EU is more likely to go through unpredictable internal and external tensions which could even estrange Europe again and end the European project.[119] That this scenario is not simply utopian was proved by the IGC in December 2003.

4. The Myths concerning the European Constitution

There are several myths which have been spread by Europsceptics and certain media in order to discredit the idea of a EU Constitution of which just the three most severe ones are briefly tackled below.

4.1. The Creation of a Super-State

For some the idea of a European Constitution is deeply troublesome because of the anxiety that a Constitution inevitably results in a super-state to which the Member States surrender their independence and sovereignty.[120] The inclusion of the principle of primacy[121] as thus seen as an indicator.[122]

Firstly, the Laeken Declaration explicitly denies such efforts and plans and moreover proclaims the protection of the Member States individu-

---

[119] Dzurinda, *ibid.*, p 3; Leicht, http://zeus.zeit.de/text/archiv/2002/10/200210_verfassgsmodelle.xml, para 10.
[120] Michael Ancram, shadow Foreign Secretary UK, said on 20 June 2004 that the treaty was "a gateway to a country called Europe", cf. A. Beatty, "Blair to expose 'EU myths'", http://www.euobserver.com of 21 June 2004.
[121] Art. I-6 CT.
[122] See "A flawed document – The EU constitution is a recipe for confusion", Leading Article in *The Times* on 19/06/2004.

ality as does Art. I-5 (1) CT.[123] Secondly, it would not be in conformity with Art. 6 (3) TEU. Thirdly, the Constitutional Treaty does not change anything and the EU lacks state-like or super-state-like features such as (i) the right to raise taxes autonomously, (ii) the autonomous right to raise a military force or (iii) full competence (*Kompetenz-Kompetenz*) which is the opposite to the principle of conferral.[124] Fourthly, the principle of primacy merely restates the current legal position.[125]

Consequently, a Constitution will not arouse a European Super-State since the Member States only pool some of their sovereignty.

4.2. European Constitution swallows National Constitutions

Some fears are based on the rumour that a EU-Constitution would possibly undermine the respective national constitutions. Against this assertion one only has to have a look at the Federal Republic of Germany where the federal basic law (the *Grundgesetz*) co-exists with the constitutions of the *Länder*. Both the constitutions of the Member States and the EU-Constitution have their own source of legitimacy and therefore, though their complementarity, co-exist in a multilevel constitutional system.[126]

---

[123] *Laeken Declaration*, Chapter I subheading "The expectations of Europe's citizens".
[124] MacCormick, *op. cit.* n 103, p 21.
[125] As developed in *Costa v ENEL*.
[126] Dutheil de la Rochère / Pernice, *op. cit.* n 17, p 72; Pernice, (2003) *FCE Spezial 1/03 Speech at the Urania Berlin*, pp 7, 14 f.; Thym, *op. cit.* n 108, p 155.

4.3. Extensive EU-Powers over Foreign Affairs, Defence and Employment Laws

Further concerns are about the EU gaining extensive powers over foreign, defence, and employment laws through the Constitutional Treaty.[127] True is that there are institutional changes. Nonetheless there are no new powers on defence which remains the preserve of the nation states. The document makes clear that there will only be majority voting in foreign affairs in the implementation of policies already unanimously agreed by all 25 Member States. Due to British efforts explanations have been agreed on which shall ensure that the Charter on Fundamental Rights does not create any new employment rights.[128] They do not have the status of law but serve as tools of interpretation and the ECJ will have to pay due regard to these explanations. Thus, powers of the EU will not be extended significantly in these areas by the EU-Constitution.

5. Intermediate Conclusion to Part I

The EU is capable of having a constitution even in the form of a constitutional treaty. Despite already possessing a functional or implicit

---

[127] "EU Constitution – the main points", 19 June 2004 *The Daily Mail*, http://www.dailymail.co.uk/pages/live/articles/news/news.html?in_article_id=30 7249&in_page_id=1770, on Web August 2004.

[128] Cf. *Declaration concerning the explanations relating to the Charter of Fundamental Rights*, Addendum 2 to CIG 87/04 Declarations to be annexed to the Final Act of the Intergovernmental Conference and the Final Act; Preamble of Part II of the Constitutional Treaty.

constitution the necessity for a formal constitutional document is inevitable.

PART II

A SUCCESSFUL ADVANCE ON THE TREATY SYSTEM ?

Part II
A Successful Advance on the Treaty System ?

"L'Europe ne se fera pas d'un coup, ni dans une construction d'ensemble: elle se fera par des réalisation concrètes, créant d'abord une solidarité de fait."
(Robert Schuman)[129]

The arguments mentioned in the previous chapter are not sufficient on their own in order to underpin the essential need to ratify the Constitutional Treaty. Ratification is only sensible if the agreed Constitutional Treaty is an advance on the current Treaty system plus a promising and solid legal document.

1. Advantages and Disadvantages of written Constitutions

Written constitutions may serve as a catalyst and give impetus to the process of identity-building among a certain group of people as was shown in the foregoing chapter. Apart from that a written constitution makes the basic rights and rules of an entity, organization or state more transparent, more tangible and clearer to the people concerned. Moreover, constitutions are meant to be stable and they usually are entrenched, i.e. can only be amended by special procedures.[130]

---

[129] "Europe will not be made all at once, or according to a single, general plan. It will be built through concrete achievements, which first create a de facto solidarity." Robert Schuman (1886-1963), "Declaration of 9 May 1950", http://www.robert-schuman.org/robert-schuman/declaration2.htm.
[130] Raz, *op. cit.* n 13, pp 153 f.

However, too rigid constitutions might obstruct further development and lead to inertia of the concerned entity.[131] Accordingly, this would be troublesome if the Constitutional Treaty was not an advance on the current legal system of the EU.

2. Determination and Assessment of Success

Decisive parameters for the assessment of the success of the agreed Constitutional Treaty are twofold: The CT has to (i) fulfill the acknowledged functions of common constitutions[132] and (ii) achieve the objectives set out in the Declarations of Nice and Laeken.

3. Declarations of Nice and Laeken

The Commission's White Paper on Governance[133] certainly must be regarded as the inspiration for the later Declarations of Nice and Laeken. That document emphasized five principles which are important for good governance: Openness, participation, accountability, effectiveness and coherence.[134] The Declarations in 2001 focussed on four central issues: The (i) enhancement of democratic legitimacy,

---

[131] For a exact definition of the terms rigid and flexible constitutions see Garner, *op. cit.* n 12, p 306; According to Art. IV-443 to IV-444 DT is the Constutional Treaty a rigid document.
[132] As described in Part I.1.1.
[133] COM 2001 / 428 *White Paper on Governance*, http://europa.eu.int/eur-lex/en/com/cnc/2001/ com2001_0428en01.pdf , on Web July 2004.
[134] *White Paper on Governance*, p 10.

transparency and effectiveness, (ii) new allocation and delimitation of powers and competences, (iii) simplification and reorganization of the Treaties and (iv) the inclusion of the Charter of Fundamental Rights in the basic treaty of the EU.[135]

The achievement of these objectives is scrutinized in the following.

4. Simplification and Reorganization of the Treaties

This part explains the meaning of these terms and assesses whether and how the objectives were achieved or even may be flawed.

4.1. Meaning of Simplification and Reorganization

The complex pillar-system established by the Treaty of Maastricht in 1992 is source of confusion on both the international and intra-communitarian level. Due to that fact simplification and reorganization of the Union's Treaty system was desperately needed.

In this context simplification especially means the revision and correction of the distinction between the EU and the EC, possibly by the creation of a single legal entity[136]. Moreover, simplification should be achieved by a simplification and reduction of the Union's instruments.[137] The reorganization, as a second step, was intended to divide

---

[135] *Nice Treaty Declaration No 23*, para 5 f; *Laeken Declaration*, Chapter II.
[136] *Laeken Declaration*, Chapter II; Kokott / Rüth, (2003) *40 C.M.L.Rev.* 1322.
[137] *Laeken Declaration*, Chapter II subheading "Simplification of the Union's intruments".

the legal provisions into a basic (or fundamental) and a less-basic (or more procedural) part.[138]

These measures were believed to render the Union more transparent and comprehensible which would help to regain the European citizens' trust in the EU.[139]

4.2. One Union

The Constitutional Treaty merges the Communities and the Union[140], bases the EU on a single legal document by repealing the current Treaties[141] and provides the EU with legal personality under domestic and international law[142] At present, the actual practice only allows to conclude an implicit legal personality of the EU.[143] Additionally, the Charter of Fundamental Rights becomes integrated and clearifies its legal status.[144]

These steps certainly contribute to the enhancement of effectiveness, legal certainty, transparency and heightens the profile of the Union as desired by the Laeken Declaration.

---

[138] *Laeken Declaration*, Chapter II subheading "Towards a constitution for European citizens".
[139] Kokott / Rüth, (2003) *40 C.M.L.Rev.* 1322.
[140] Arts I-1, IV-438 CT, the European Union replaces the present European Communities and European Union.
[141] Art. IV-437 CT plus five protocols which form an integral part of the Constitutional Treaty, Art. IV-442 CT.
[142] Art. I-6 CT.
[143] Kokott / Rüth, (2003) *40 C.M.L.Rev.* 1323.
[144] Part II CT.

4.3. The (unfinished) Merger of the Pillars

The Constitutional Treaty merges the current three pillars[145] but maintains special procedures in the fields of foreign policy, security and defence.[146]

The area of freedom, security and justice[147] will follow the Community method, i.e. qualified majority applies in the majority of its areas, different legal instruments are abolished and the area is subject to the full jurisdiction of the Court of Justice. Only where national interests are, according to the Member States, at stake, legal review is excluded.[148] This is a clear extension of legal review compared to the *status quo*.[149]

In the area of CFSP the current exclusion of the Court's jurisdiction[150] will continue with some exceptions.[151] Moreover, the ordinary Community decision-making procedures will not apply,[152] unanimity will remain the general rule[153] and European laws and framework laws will be excluded.[154]

---

[145] Art. IV-437 and 438 CT.
[146] Current second pillar known as Common Foreign and Security Policy (CFSP); Commission, (2004) "Summary of the agreement on the Constitutional Treaty", 1-5 at p 2.
[147] Current third pillar of the EU.
[148] Art. III-377 CT.
[149] Cf. Art. 68 EC, Art. 35 TEU.
[150] Arts 46, 47 TEU.
[151] Cf. Art. III-376 CT.
[152] Art. I-40 (2)-(4) CT.
[153] Arts I-40 (6), III-300 CT.
[154] Arts I-40 (6), III-294 (3) CT.

Further, EURATOM will last as independent legal entity.[155]

Whereas the current third pillar is formally incorporated and materially merged with the first pillar, the second pillar remains seperated and distinct from the principles and procedures provided by the Constitutional Treaty.[156] The European legal order has more or less solely been extended to the area of freedom, justice and security. However, a huge step has been made towards a single legal entity by the full inclusion of the second pillar, although the simplification could have been more far-reaching by an unconditional subjection of the second pillar to the Community method and jurisdiction. However, as an integral part of the Constitution, CFSP is subject to fundamental principles and not completely out of the general structure of the Union.[157]

5. Analysis of specific Parts of the Constitutional Treaty

This section looks at crucial parts of the Constitutional Treaty and examines whether they are advantageous compared to, if existing at all, the current provisions.

5.1. The Union of the People

As already the Declaration of Nice mentioned, the Union has to be brought closer to its citizens.[158] The attempt to achieve this goal is

---

[155] *Protocol Amending the EURATOM Treaty.*
[156] Kokott / Rüth, (2003) *40 C.M.L.Rev.* 1326.
[157] Lenaerts / Gerard, (2004) *29 E.L.Rev.*, p 308.
[158] *Nice Treaty Declaration No 23*, para 6.

visible in different areas of the Draft Constitution. Not only Member States or their peoples are the legitimizing authority but also their (Union) citizens.[159] This is stated in the preamble as well as in Art. I-1 CT. Also, the European Parliament (EP) now represents the citizens and no longer merely the "peoples" of Europe.[160] In addition, Part I, Title VI of the Constitution deals with the democratic life of the Union and constantly mentions the "citizens" as its basis.[161] The citizens may even enforce the Commission to submit a legislative proposal via a petition.[162] The latter has been criticized as a "gimmick" that allows minority interests representing less than a third of one percent of the Union population to hijack Commission legislative resources.[163] Contrary to that point of view, this rather indicates a paradigm shift allocating the citizens a vital role in the constitutional framework of the EU[164] and softening the strictly representative character of European democracy.

5.2. The "Exit-Clause"

The unprecedent "Exit-Clause" of Art. I-60 CT ends the mystery of how to withdraw from the EU.[165] "The Union shall negotiate and con-

---

[159] Editorial Comment, "The sixteen articles: On a way to a European Constitution", (2003) 40 C.M.L.Rev. 267-277 at p 270; Pernice, (2003) FCE Spezial 1/03 Speech at the Urania Berlin, p 16.
[160] Compare Arts I-20 (2), I-46 (2) CT to Arts 189, 190 EC.
[161] Cf. Arts I-45, I-46 (2)-(4), I-47 (1), I-50 (3) CT.
[162] According to procedure laid down in Art. I-47 (4) CT.
[163] A. Arnull / D. Chalmers, "Editorial: A Constitution whose bottle is definitely half-full and not half-empty", (2003) 28 E.L.Rev. 449-450 at p 449.
[164] Cf. Pernice, (2003) FCE Spezial 1/03 Speech at the Urania Berlin, p 16.
[165] M. Dougan, "The Convention's Draft Constitutional Treaty: A 'Tidying-Up Exercise' that Needs Some Tidying-Up of Its Own", (2003) Online Paper 27/03 The Federal Trust for Education and Research, 1-18 at p 8.

clude an agreement with the state"[166] considering the withdrawal recognizes the Union's autonomous status. EU-law separates itself from public international law, which allows withdrawal from a treaty only "by consent of all the [contracting] parties".[167] Contrary to that procedure, the withdrawal would be concluded by an agreement "by the Council, acting by qualified majority, after obtaining the consent of the European Parliament".[168] Consequently, the "Exit-Clause" serves as an example of how the EU has become an autonomous entity different from classic international organizations, not depending on international law.[169] Besides it proves that the EU will not become a superstate.

5.3. Fundamental Principles, Rights and Values

Different parts and provisions of the Constitution implement principles, values and rights which shall have fundamental legal status in the Union.

Firstly, the present, fundamental values which are spread all over the Treaties[170] now can be found "in form of a brilliant synthesis

---

[166] Art. I-60 (2) CT.
[167] Arts I-54, I-64-65 *Vienna Convention on the Law of Treaties*.
[168] Art. I-60 (2) CT.
[169] Cf. Lenaerts / Gerard, (2004) 29 *E.L.Rev.* 306.
[170] Cf. Part II.2.3. (n 95) of this thesis: Citizen's rights Art. 12, 17 ff. EC; principles of openness, closeness to the citizens and solidarity among Member States and their peoples (Art. 1 TEU); principle of sustainable development (Art. 2 TEU); elimination of inequalities and the promotion of equality between men and women (Arts 3 (2) and 141 EC); principle of subsidiarity (Art. 5 EC); the protection of the environment (Art. 6 EC), the prohibition of discrimination based on sex, racial or ethnic origin, religion or belief, disability, age or sexual orientation (Art. 13 EC).

of fundamental principles and goals on which the Union is built"[171] in the Constitution.[172] Just at the IGC in Brussels it was decided that the Article on the Symbols of the Union should be transferred from Part IV to Part I of the Constitution, resembling national constitutions.[173]

Secondly, the Charter of Fundamental Rights has become an integral, legally binding part of the Constitution.[174] It contents common European constitutional traditions and values.[175] As legally binding part the ECJ is entitled to review according to Arts I-29, II-107, III-365 CT. Unfortunately, the Constitution does not provide a special legal remedy similar to those in some Member States.[176] This would have been an extra feature strengthening the public confidence in the EU-Constitution.

The aforementioned elements are hugely important for the building of a common identity, confidence in the Constitution and increasing its value as the basic document of the EU. It contributes to legal certainty and fulfils one of the main functions of constitutions: The guarantee and protection of fundamental and civil rights, the status of the citizens and definition of common values. It showes once more that the status of the Union's citizens has been improved. Moreover, the incorporation of the Charter emphasizes the difference between international

---

[171] Lenaerts / Gerard, (2004) *29 E.L.Rev.* 316.
[172] Part II Title I-II and Part III Title I CT.
[173] E.g. Art. 22 *Grundgesetz (GG)* determines the colours of the German National Flag.
[174] As Part II CT; cf. Art. I-9 CT; Lenaerts /Gerard, (2004) *29 E.L.Rev.* 317.
[175] Cf. Recital 1 Preamble of Part II CT.
[176] Art. 93 (1) Nr. 4a GG *"Verfassungsbeschwerde"* in Germany or *"Recurso de amparo"* in Spain.

organizations and the EU: The former does not know the protection of fundamental rights.[177] It expresses that the Union "places the individual at the heart of its activities".[178]

5.4. Decision-Making in the (European) Council

In Brussels 2004 the Member States finally agreed on a definition of qualified majority voting for decision-making in the Council which will replace the current system according to Art. 205 EC and put aside the unbalanced agreement reached in Nice.[179] According to the new qualified majority procedure decisions will be taken on the basis of double majority: It requires 55% of the Member States representing 65% of the population.[180] A blocking minority can be formed by four States.[181]

Following to that, qualified majority voting has become the ordinary procedure for the adoption of European laws and framework laws in the Council[182] being extended from 34 policy areas to 70 areas,[183] including the area of freedom, security and justice.[184]

---

[177] Pernice, (2003) *FCE Spezial 1/03 Speech at the Urania Berlin*, p 17.
[178] Recital 2 of the Preamble Part II CT.
[179] Cf. Art. 3 *Protocol on the Enlargement of the European Union*.
[180] Art. I-25 (1) CT; at least 15 Member States are required.
[181] Art. I-25 (1) CT.
[182] Cf. Arts I-23 (3), I-34, III-396 CT.
[183] Commission, (2004) "Summary of the agreement on the Constitutional Treaty", p 4; Ferguson, "Europe gets my vote" (2004) in *The Guardian*, http://election.guardian.co.uk/eu/comment/0,9236, 1249455,00.html.
[184] Cf. Arts I-14 (2) (j), III-396 CT.

Nevertheless, unanimity, or the so-called "national veto",[185] is retained in most areas of the CFSP sector,[186] some international agreements[187] and social policy,[188] and especially in the field of taxation.[189] Laws on own resources,[190] the financial perspectives[191] and revisions of the Constitution[192] itself also have to be adopted unanimously.

Unfortunately, the signatories did not extend the simple or qualified majority voting system to the important areas of taxation and CFSP due to the UK's "red lines". This would certainly have enabled the EU to pursue more independently a policy based on its own resources while shrugging off the never ending debate about net contributors and recipients and to found an even "thicker" European constitutional regime.[193] Nonetheless, the introduction of double majority is a crucial constitutional step forward: It is an appreciation and recognition of a basic principle of democracy, simple and comprehensible for the citizens and it reflects the fact that the EU represents the Mem-

---

[185] Ferguson, (2004) *The Guardian*, http://election.guardian.co.uk/eu/comment/0,9236,1249455,00.html; "An EU constitutional primer – What it all means", (2004) *371 The Economist*, p 42.
[186] Cf. Art. III-300 (1) CT; However, a move towards generalised majority voting in this area is provided for but its implementation seems unlikely as it requires an unanimous decision by the European Council, Arts I-40 (7), III-300 (3) CT.
[187] Cf. Arts III-315 (4), III-325 (8) CT.
[188] Cf. Arts III-210 (3), III-212 (2) CT.
[189] Cf. Art. III-171 CT.
[190] Cf. Art. I-54 (3) CT.
[191] Art. I-55 (2) CT.
[192] Art. IV-443 (3) CT which provides for "common accord".
[193] Lenaerts / Gerard, (2004) *29 E.L.Rev.* 320; Thym, *op. cit.* n 108, p 176; G. Verhofstadt, "The new European Constitution – from Laeken to Rome", *Humboldt-Reden zu Europa Speech at the Humboldt-University Berlin*, 1-13 at p 6.

ber States itself as well as the citizens.[194] "The Community method has been streamlined, strengthened and [...] democratised."[195]

5.5. Competences and Powers

According to the Declarations of Nice and Laeken the main issues in regard of the Union's competences were the "more precise delimitation of powers between the European Union and the Member States, reflecting the principle of subsidiarity"[196] and the clearer, more functional and better reorganization and division of competence.

Articles I-11 to I-18 CT lay down the rules for the exercise of the Union's competences. Art. I-11 CT states several principles that govern the division of competences while Articles I-12 to I-18 CT abstractly names the competences.[197] These competences are linked to specific legal bases of Part III of the Constitution[198] which determine the scope of the competences.[199]

5.5.1. The Competences

There are three main categories of powers: Exclusive, shared and supporting competences.[200] Additionally, the Union has the power to

---

[194] Cf. Peters, (2004) *41 C.M.L.Rev.* 58.
[195] K. Hughes, "A new division of power in the EU ?", (2004) *EU Constitution Project Newsletter Special Issue July*, 1-16 at p 13.
[196] *Nice Treaty Declaration No 23*, para 5.
[197] Principles of conferral, subsidiarity and proportionality.
[198] M. Dougan, "The Convention's Draft Constitutional Treaty: bringing Europe closer to its lawyers?", (2003) *28 E.L.Rev.* 763-793 at p 769.
[199] Art. I-12 (6) CT.
[200] Art. I-12 (1)-(2), (5) CT defines the respective areas of competences.

promote and coordinate economic and employment policies, and competences to frame and implement the CFSP.[201]

Articles I-13 and I-17 CT provide exhaustive lists and Art. I-14 produces an indicative list of the respective areas of competence concerned.[202] Unfortunately, the coordination of economic policies and the CFSP seem to fall outside these general categories due to their peculiar and unique status, thus slighty interfere with the overall concept of Part I Title III.

5.5.2. The Principle of Subsidiarity

As the aforementioned articles, with exception of Art. I-13 DT, merely explain "when" the Union is entitled to make use of its powers, the decisive question of "if" and "to what extent" is answered by the principle of subsidiarity.[203] The enforcement of the principle is based on Art. I-11 (1), (3) and two protocols which provide either political or judicial procedures.[204] These provisions shall guarantee the successful application of the principle of subsidiarity by means of an "*ex ante* monitoring" and "early warning system".[205] The basic idea of this system is to

---

[201] Art. I-12 (3)-(4) CT.
[202] G. Davies, "The post-Laeken division of competences", (2003) *28 E.L.Rev.* 686-698 at p 688. Dougan, (2003) *28 E.L.Rev.* 769.
[203] Cf. Dougan, (2003) *28 E.L.Rev.* 767; Pernice, (2003) *FCE Spezial 1/03 Speech at the Urania Berlin*, p 17.
[204] CIG 87/04 Addendum 1: *Protocol on the role of Member States' national Parliaments in the European Union*; *Protocol on the application of the principles of subsidiarity and proportionality*; the protocols are an integral part of the Constitutional Treaty, IV-442 CT.
[205] Dougan, (2003) *28 E.L.Rev.* 767; Pernice, (2003) *FCE Spezial 1/03 Speech at the Urania Berlin*, p 18; cf. Arts 2-4 *Protocol on the role of Member States' na-*

oblige the Commission to send all ist legislative proposals to the national parliaments [... which] could then issue reasoned opinions, within a six-week period, expressing disagreement [...] specifically on the grounds that they do not comply with the principle of subsidiarity.[206]

By doing so the national parliaments may enforce a review of the proposal.[207] Moreover, acts of the Union may be challenged before the ECJ by a Member State or on behalf of a national parliament as long as there exists a national legal basis for doing so.[208]

5.5.3. The Flexibility Clause

Further, the Laeken Declaration remarked that "the Union must continue to be able to react to fresh challenges and developments [while it keeps ist ability] to explore new policy areas".[209] This task is currently fulfilled by Arts 95, 308 EC. Art. I-18 CT is to some extent the former articles equivalent. However, its potential scope is wider than that of Art. 308 EC since the application is no longer linked to the operation of the common market.[210] In spite of that theoretical possibility it seems highly unlikely that the provisions will gain significant relevance for several reasons[211]: (i) Art. I-18 (1) requires an unanimous

---

tional Parliaments in the European Union; Arts 3-6 *Protocol on the application of the principles of subsidiarity and proportionality.*

[206] Dougan, (2003) 28 *E.L.Rev.* 767.
[207] Art. 6 *Protocol on the application of the principles of subsidiarity and proportionality.*
[208] *Ibid.* Art. 7.
[209] *Laeken Declaration*, Chapter II subheading "A better division and definition of competence in the European Union".
[210] Davies, (2003) 28 *E.L.Rev* 688; Dougan, (2003) 28 *E.L.Rev.* 766.
[211] Contrary opinion Davies, (2003) 28 *E.L.Rev* 688 f.

decision by the Council, (ii) it further imposes two prerequisites[212] and (iii) Art. I-18 (3) prohibits harmonisation in cases where the Constitution excludes such a possibility. Thus it does not seem to be suitable for major, even unforeseen (constitutional) challenges as the article is simply far too rigid and paved with safeguards.[213] At least, the respect principle of conferral is guaranteed.[214]

5.5.4. Intermediate Conclusion

All in all, the objectives set out in the Laeken Declaration have been achieved: Competences are clearly and systematically named and listed in a single title of the Constitution which may arguably be regarded as a major constitutional innovation.[215] The principle of subsidiarity, as a key to a widely accepted EU-Constitution[216], is reflected in an elaborated procedure involving national parliaments to an increased extent in EU-legislation. By doing so the "early warning system" places the role of the guardian exactly at the potential victims of infringements affecting national competences. It is a necessary tool which allows Member States and its Regions to hold their grounds on the internal and global level.[217] Solely the incapability of national parliaments to block a proposal must be criticized, as must the complexity

---

[212] "[...] prove necessary, within the framework of the policies defined in Part III, to attain one of the objectives set by the Constitution, and the Constitution has not provided the necessary powers [...]".

[213] However, Art. 308 EC is phrased similarly but only had to deal with 15 Member States.

[214] Cf. Kokott / Rüth, (2003) *40 C.M.L.Rev.* 1341.

[215] Cf. A. Dashwood, "The Relationship between the Member States and the European Union / European Community", (2004) *41 C.M.L.Rev.* 355-381 at p 370.

[216] Teufel, (2003) *FCE 3/03 Speech at the Humboldt-University Berlin*

[217] Cf. Schmuck, (2003) *279 Informationen zur politischen Bildung* 57.

of the procedure with its unforgiving timetables which might overburden national parliaments.[218] Notwithstanding these shortcomings, the reorganization of competences achieved to meet the significant objective of clarification and transparency, especially when compared to the *status quo*.[219]

5.6. The new Institutional Order[220]

The probably most disputed and most controversial object of the new Constitution was the institutional reform of the EU.[221] The Laeken Declaration in this respect raised three core tasks: To increase the democratic legitimacy and transparency of the institutions; to integrate national Parliaments into European integration in order to further increase the democratic legitimacy of the Union; and to improve the efficiency of the decision-making and the workings of the institutions, in particular in the lights of the forthcoming enlargement.[222]

As the second task, due to overlappings with the competence issue, has been dealt with in the previous section this part focuses on the remaining tasks.

---

[218] Cf. Davies, (2003) *28 E.L.Rev* 695.
[219] Cf. Davies, (2003) *28 E.L.Rev* 697; Dougan, (2003) *Online Paper 27/03 The Federal Trust for Education and Research*, p 7.
[220] See Appendix 3 "Main Reforms to the Institutional Framework"
[221] Cf. Kokott / Rüth, (2003) *40 C.M.L.Rev.* 1330.
[222] *Laeken Declaration*, Chapter II subheading "More democracy, transparency and efficiency in the European Union".

5.6.1. Increasing Democratic Legitimacy and Transparency

The Constitutional Treaty, in principle, maintains the present institutional design.[223] It is justified to state that the Constitution, by defining the functions of each institution[224] and providing for a better delimitation of powers within the instutional triangle, uphelds the traditional concept but also facilitates its understanding. Moreover, the EU-Constitution draws a clear distinction between legislative and non-legislative acts helping to distinguish between actions of the legislative from those of the executive.[225] The co-decision procedure has been upgraded to the ordinary legislative procedure[226] by putting the European Parliament on equal footing with the Council[227] which unquestionably supports and enhances the democratic legitimacy of the Union's legislative acts. Regrettably, no agreement could be achieved in some sensitive areas for the Member States, especially due to the UK's "red lines", where exceptions are made from the aforementioned rule.[228]

Considering this, it becomes obvious that the new Constitition is not consequent to the utmost extent. However, a major overhaul of the institutional order would have been premature and could very likely have endangered the acception of the Constitution as well as the EU itself. Therefore, it seems much more reasonable to bring the necessary institutional reform and adjustment's of the Union's institutional archi-

---

[223] Kokott / Rüth, (2003) *40 C.M.L.Rev.* 1331.
[224] Arts I-20 (1), I-23 (1) and I-26 (1) CT.
[225] Cf. Dougan, (2003) *28 E.L.Rev.* 767.
[226] Arts I-34 (1) and III-396 CT.
[227] Cf. Peters, (2004) *41 C.M.L.Rev.* 49.
[228] Arts I-34 (2) and e.g. III-171; III-173; III-176 CT.

tecture in a progressive form or, in other words, step by step, rather than "by a single 'constitutional stroke'".[229]

5.6.2. Improving Efficiency

As the institutional design was developed for a Union with less than half of today's number of Member States the Constitution has to provide solutions which contributes to the smooth, continous and efficient functioning of the EU. In this context the introduction of the post of a permanent President of the European Council, the creation of the post of a Foreign Affairs Minister and the restructuring of the Commission deserve the most attention.

Due to the permanently growing Union the rotation system could not be preserved[230] and Art. I-22 (1) CT provides for a permanent President for two and a half years. Some scholars fear that a permanent President might interfere with the role of the Commission President or with that of the Foreign Affairs Minister.[231] This gloomy anticipation cannot be accepted as the Constitutional Treaty does not extend the President's functions compared to the *status quo*.[232] Thus, a prolonged term and a permanent, full-time Presidency are more likely to guarantee a more efficient and continous conducting of the Council's work than a, to formulate it provocative, permanently changing part-time

---

[229] Kokott / Rüth, (2003) *40 C.M.L.Rev.* 1331.
[230] According to the present system under Art. 203 EC each of the 25 Member States would hold the Presidency only once every thirteen years.
[231] Cf. Kokott / Rüth, (2003) *40 C.M.L.Rev.* 1337.
[232] Cf. Art. I-22 (2) CT, which merely codifies the tasks currently exercised by the rotating Presidency.

President who at the same time is the Head of a Member State's Government.[233]

The Council of Ministers will continue to have a rotating Presidency[234] unless the Foreign Affairs Council which will be presided by the Minister of Foreign Affairs.[235] Further, the Foreign Affairs Minister represents the Union externally and conducts its common foreign and security policy as well as the common security and defence policy – as mandated by the Council.[236]

Paying attention to the reform of the Commission it is necessary to mention that "for the sake of the efficient functioning of the College the maintenance or even reduction of the [before 1 May 2004] current number is required".[237] However, the Commission will maintain its current composition until 2014. Thereafter, the number of commissioners will be reduced to two thirds of the number of Member States, selected on the basis of an equal rotation system.[238]

With regard to the permanent President of the Council, the Foreign Affairs Minister and the President of the Commission the Union will hopefully finally have a recognisable "face" (or rather three),

---

[233] The President of the reformed European Council may not hold a national mandate anymore, Art. I-22 (3) CT.
[234] Cf. Art. I-24 (7) CT.
[235] Cf. Art. I-28 (1), (3) CT.
[236] Art. I-28 (2) CT.
[237] Kokott / Rüth, (2003) *40 C.M.L.Rev.* 1338.
[238] Cf. Art. I-26 (6) CT.

giving the Union the possibility to become more popular, representing its Member States with "one voice".[239]

As far as the Commission is concerned several aspects have to be criticised: (i) The reduction of Commissioners should not have been postponed to 2014, endangering the EU of 25 to become unflexible, (ii) even after 2014 the Commission will consist of 16 or even more Commissioners[240] which means that (iii) the number of Commissioners will even have been increased in comparison to the pre-enlargement era. Nonetheless, the solution by the Constitution is better than the current procedure with 25 Commissioners.[241] That solution, at least, expresses and proves that Member States slowly but surely overcome their omnipresent national "egoism" concerning the Commission and maybe even of the EU.

Thus, the courses for a more efficient functioning of the institutions have been set – the fulfilment of the objectives now depends on the responsible individuals.

5.7. Simplification of Legal Instruments

Another key component of the Laeken Declaration was the simplification of the Union's instruments and procedures in order to tackle the transparency problem.[242] The EU-Constitution reduces the number of instruments from currently 16 to five, abondons the separate legal tools for the former second and third pillar areas, and abolishes the co-

---

[239] Cf. Di Fabio, (2004) 5 G.L.J. para 8.
[240] Depending on the number of future accessions of (Member) States.
[241] Current from 1 November 2004 when the new Commission's term commenced.
[242] *Laeken Declaration*, Title II subheading "Simplification of the Unions instruments".

operation procedure.[243] Additionally, the document introduces a formal hierarchy by dividing between legislative and non-legislative (executive) acts and ends the "obscure patchwork of norms with ill-defined scope, legal effects and institutional origin".[244] The new set of instruments is clearly and fully named in the Constitution:[245] Legislative acts are divided into European laws,[246] which correspond to current regulations,[247] and European framework laws,[248] which correspond to current directives.[249] European regulations[250] and European decisions,[251] which roughly correspond to current decisions,[252] are non-legislative acts.[253] However, "in specific cases duly justified" the Council retains the right for implementing legally binding Union acts.[254] Contrary to that, the newly incorporated category of delegated European regulations[255] might be seen as a positive reaction to the urge to combine legitimacy and democratic accountability with the necessary flexibility and efficiency.[256]

---

[243] Cf. Kokott / Rüth, (2003) *40 C.M.L.Rev.* 1338; Peters, (2004) *41 C.M.L.Rev.* 65.
[244] Lenaerts / Gerard, (2004) 29 *E.L.Rev.* 309; cf. Peters, (2004) *41 C.M.L.Rev.* 65; for a table on the new hierarchy of norms see Dougan, (2003) *28 E.L.Rev.* 781.
[245] Art. I-33 CT.
[246] Arts I-33 (1), I-34 CT.
[247] Dougan, (2003) *28 E.L.Rev.* 782.
[248] Arts I-33 (1), I-34 CT.
[249] Dougan, (2003) *28 E.L.Rev.* 782.
[250] Arts I-33 (1), I-35 CT.
[251] Arts I-33 (1), I-35 CT.
[252] Dougan, (2003) *28 E.L.Rev.* 783.
[253] Further, the Union's legal instruments are completed by non-binding recommendations and opinions.
[254] Arts I-37 (2), I-40 CT, i.e. mainly in the area of CFSP.
[255] Art. I-36 CT.
[256] Kokott / Rüth, (2003) *40 C.M.L.Rev.* 1342; Lenaerts / Koenen, (2004) *E.L.Rev.* p 311.

Although not perfect in all details, the simplification improves the comprehensibility of legislative instruments of the Union, has the capability to (hopefully) remove the present barrier to public understanding and wide-spread acceptance and thus an enhanced democratic legitimacy of the Union.[257]

6. Intermediate Conclusion

To summarize the points in this part it may, and rightly so, be stated that the Constitutional Treaty, in comparison to the current amalgam of Treaties and jurisprudence, is a success in the sense of the objectives stated in the Laeken Declaration, advantageous, innovative to some extent, reduces the legitimacy deficit and, despite its dimensions, distinctly more user-friendly. Thus, ratification would not merely be justified on grounds of the symbolical value of having a Constitution but also on grounds of the advantages of the legal value of the document.

---

[257] Cf. Kokott / Rüth, (2003) *40 C.M.L.Rev.* 1342 f.

PART III

BRUSSELS 2004: EFFECTS, AFTERMATH AND REFERENDA

Part III

Brussels 2004: Effects, Aftermath and Referenda

"Our Constitution ... is called a democracy because power is in the hands not of a minority but of the greatest number."
(Thucydides)[258]

Since the Heads of Governments of the Member States during IGC in Brussels, after the miserable failure in December 2003, on 18-19 June 2004 have finally agreed on the Constitutional Treaty for Europe, it is now interesting to ask which effects that summit and its outcome might have on the EU, what problems are likely to occur during the ratification period and how these could possibly be tackled. In brief, Part III also reflects on the reasons which made an agreement possible among Member States which were so deeply divided just half a year earlier.

1. Finally an Agreement

On 19 June 2004 the Member States finally agreed on the Constitutional Treaty which will be signed at 29 October 2004.[259] After the de-

---

[258] Thucydides (471-400 B.C.), History of the Peleponnesian War, Part II, 37 (referring to the Constitution of Athens under Pericles); This quote was the 'motto' of the Draft Treaty establishing a Constitution for Europe in its Preamble. However, the IGC of Brussels in June 2004 dropped the quote from the final version (CIG 87/04).

[259] Cf. H. Mahony, "Constitution to be signed end of October", http://www.euobserver.com/?aid=16859&sid=18, on Web July 2004.

sastrous outcome of the summit of December 2003 such a relatively sudden accord was highly unlikely[260] and only possible due to several factors:

First, the Irish Presidency showed skilled diplomacy, in contrast to Italy's Prime Minister Berlusconi in 2003, by arranging formal intergovernmental talks on ministerial level where most obstacles to an agreement could already be removed. Then the Presidency issued a paper with a proposal how to break the deadlock.[261] Second, the return to power of Spain's Socialist Party signalled an immediate shift towards compromise which also resulted in Poland easing its position concerning the new double majority system.[262] In this point, France and Germany stuck rigidly to the proposal of the Convention. Third, several "emergency brakes" have been installed, e.g. in the area of CFSP or internal policies.[263] Further, mainly the U.K.'s so-called "red lines" were not touched, i.e. a national "veto" was maintained in the areas of taxation, CFSP and social policy,[264] which otherwise certainly had meant a no-vote. Fourth, the train bombings of Madrid on 11 March 2004 definitely opened the eyes of the European leaders that only a strong and united Europe could cope with comparable threats.

---

[260] Swedens Head of Government Göran Persson after the IGC in December 2003: he expected the next serious negotitions under the Presidency of Luxembourg in 2005.

[261] Cf. H. Mahony, "Countdown to final Constitution talks begins", http://www.euobserver.com/?aid=16607&sid=9, on Web July 2004.

[262] A. Beatty, "Spain shows its hand in Constitution debate", http://www.euobserver.com/?aid=15597&sid=9, on Web July 2004; H. Mahony, "Movement on voting issue in Constitution", http://www.euobserver.com/?aid=16223&sid=9, on Web July 2004.

[263] Cf. Arts III-136 (2), III-270 (3), 271 (3) CT.

[264] Cf. Arts III-171, III-210 (3), III-212 (2), III-300 CT.

Fifth, the smallest Member States received a modest increase in the minimum number of seats in the European Parliament.

2. Strengthened or Weakened – the Effects of the Agreement

The lengthy and at the final summit sometimes fierce battle in several key areas of the Constitution evoked a split evaluation in the international media:[265] Some newspapers declared the agreement on a Constitution as a milestone and Europe's greatest leap in history, a honourable compromise and proclaimed that an important hurdle had been cleared. Others emphasized that the British or even the bloc of blockers had succeeded in slowing down the process of integration, stating that the compromise would cause Europe to struggle to make an impact on world politics and being "able to speak with one voice only when all voices are saying the same [...] which would be quite rare".[266] To me it seems that the Constitution give impetus to Europe, strengthening its progress and drive. The text is historical and likely to reinforce the Union's coherence and its place in the world. However, without the strong will to overcome the divergences between (some) Member States the Constitution will not be enough.

---

[265] See Appendix 4 "Press Reviews".
[266] P. Reynolds, "Constitution a hard-won compromise", http://www.news.bbc.co.uk/go/pr/fr/-/1/hi/world/europe/3820557.stm, on Web July 2004.

3. The Aftermath OR The Problem of Ratification

Now, with a final version of the Constitution agreed and soon to be signed by the Heads of State and Government a maybe even more difficult task awaits the EU: ratification.

3.1. Provisions in the European and National Constitutions

The Constitution shall be ratified according to the constitutional requirements of the Member States.[267] Depending on the country's legal and historical traditions, there are either or both of the following two types of mechanisms: (i) the "parliamentary method" and / or (ii) the "referendum method".[268] None of the Member States constitutions explicitly provides for the adoption of a European Constitution.[269]

3.2. Consequences of Non-Ratification

If the Constitution is ratified by all of the 25 Member States, it will enter into force on 1 November 2006.[270] If two years after the Constitutional Treaty has been signed one or more countries "have encountered difficulties in proceeding with ratification" while twenty Member States have completed that process, the matter will be discussed by the

---

[267] Arts IV-447 (1) CT, 48 TEU.
[268] (i) means that the Constitution is adopted following a vote by the State's parliamentary Chamber(s); (ii) means that a referendum is held in which the citizens can directly vote for or against the Constitution; see Appendix 5 "Referenda in the EU".
[269] Cf. Dutheil de la Rochère / Pernice, *op. cit.* n 17, p 59.
[270] Art. IV-447 (2) CT.

European Council.²⁷¹ If only one single state does not ratify the text the Constitution, in pure legal terms, will be thwarted, yet a political solution, including different legal consequences, would still be possible. However, it is by no means clear what the European Council will or even could decide. According to the German Chancellor Schröder "an arrangement by which the Constitution can still come into force [ought to be found]" in this case.²⁷² Possible scenarios are as follows:

3.2.1. Retry

The Council might encourage the affected states to keep trying and have another ratification campaign.²⁷³ However, this option seems unconceivable where the population of a large Member State has rejected the Constitution or at least another outcome seems to be unlikely.²⁷⁴

3.2.2. Exclusion of "Naysayers"

If the pressure for a turnround vote in a second attempt of ratification does not prove to be enough, Member States voting against the Constitution could be excluded from the EU or, alternatively, withdraw vol-

---

[271] *Declaration on the ratification of the Treaty establishing a Constitution for Europe*, Addendum 2 to CIG 87/04 Declarations to be annexed to the Final Act of the Intergovernmental Conference and the Final Act which is legally non-binding.

[272] Quotation found in R. Carter, "Schröder: Constitution even without ratification", http://euobserver.com/?aid=15336&sid=9, on Web July 2004.

[273] Cf. Matthias Wissmann, chairman of the committee for European Affairs of the German Parliament, in S. Quenett, "In Deutschland gibt es keinen Volksentscheid", *Kölner Stadt-Anzeiger* on 21 April 2004 p 5.

[274] D. Phinnemore, "And now the really difficult bit ... ratification", (2004) *EU Constitution Project Newsletter Special Issue July*, p 14.

untarily.²⁷⁵ This option would radically split Europe again into several bits and pieces.

3.2.3. Two-speed Europe

A milder course of action would be the building of a two-speed Europe: an integrationist core that accepted the Constitution and a more loosely alligned group that opts out of many political aspects of the EU. An unfavourable effect of such a *avant garde* or centre of gravity would be the separation of Europe into two parts, the creeping creation of a Union built on axes and alliances, a patchwork-union which confuses its citizens more than ever and damages the EU permanently.²⁷⁶

3.2.4. Majority decisive

Alternatively, the Constitution could still be adopted if only 20 ot of 25 Member States ratify the text if the Council determines that this 4/5-majority is sufficient and the five remaining countries despite their contrary decision have to adopt the Constitution or leave the EU.²⁷⁷ The flawed point of this idea is that this was contrary to the Member States constitutions so that these had to be amended by national parliaments first. Although a democratic solution, this option would cause more turmoil in the concerned countries than the EU would like to. Moreover, a pro-European outcome would still be uncertain.

---

²⁷⁵ Cf. German Minister of Foreign Affairs J. Fischer in an interview by N. Fried, "'In der Geschichte geht es nicht zu wie im Gesangsverein'", *Süddeutsche Zeitung* on 25 June 2004, p 8.
²⁷⁶ Cf. Hänsch, *FCE 2/04 Speech at the Humboldt-University Berlin*, p 3.
²⁷⁷ This solution is even recognized by International Law, cf. Art. 24 *Vienna Convention on the Law of the Treaties*.

3.2.5. A European Referendum

Probably one of the most promising, if not **the** most promising, and realistic proposals is that of a European-wide referendum. There are several fairly strong arguments in support of this solution: (i) Politicians, media and hence citizens would enter into a cross-boarder debate about the Constitution and while doing so acquaint themselves with the document, demask "myths" and create a genuine opinion on the texts' virtues.[278] (ii) Exploring and debating the Constitution in the whole EU would strengthen the citizens' feelings as being "European".[279] Unquestionably, this would help to further develop a supranational identity, as a catalyst for the "European awareness and constitutional consciousness. (iii) A European plebiscite on the Constitution would automatically enhance the democratic legitimacy of the document and the Union itself.[280] The citizens would be the source and the object of a European public authority.[281] It would be another brick in the ECJ's perception that the EU is more than an ordinary international organisation.

A European referendum would promote democratic values, move away from the often simply blocking principle of unanimity and prevent the EU being "hijacked" by a tiny minority or even a single state. From a strictly legal point of view referenda are expressly pro-

---

[278] Cf. Goring, (2003) *WHI-Paper 2/03 Humboldt-University Berlin*, p 13.
[279] Cf. Thym, *op. cit.* n 108, p 166.
[280] Cf. Schmuck, (2003) *279 Informationen zur politischen Bildung* 59; Thym, *op. cit.* n 108, p 169.
[281] Cf. Thym, *op. cit.* n 108, p 166.

vided for in 18 national constitutions.[282] The constitutions of Estonia and Italy expressly exclude referenda on international treaties but nonetheless both countries have already held ballots on European issues.[283] From the remaining states only Germany does not have a legal basis or recent history of referenda.[284] However, the Constitution does not prohibit referenda and might be amended. The present author's idea of a EU-wide plebiscite is to hold 25 national referenda on the same day. Nonetheless, the votes will be counted not according to national quotas but there will be only one final European result.[285] In conformity with that basis, the majority of citizens of the Union and the majority of the Member States would be required to secure ratification. The "double majority system" would guarantee equality in the weight of votes especially for small States.

Consequently, a referendum on a European-wide basis would be a huge boost for Europe in terms of democratic legitimacy, identity-building and integration as demanded by the Laeken Declaration. "There is no alternative to a referendum if there is to be better information, understanding and communication around the constitution in a modern society. [...] [T]aking part in European affairs on a regular basis increases an electorate's affinity with and support for the European

---

[282] Austria, Czech Republic, Denmark, Finland, France, Greece, Hungary, Ireland, Latvia, Lithunia, Luxembourg, Malta, Poland, Portugal, Slovakia, Slovenia, Spain and Sweden.
[283] Estonia on the EU membership in 2003, Italy on "The EC as a federal state based on European Constitution" in 1989.
[284] The UK held a referendum on a European issue in 1975, Belgium and the Netherlands already announced a referendum on the EU-Constitution.
[285] Cf. Pernice, (2003) *FCE Spezial 1/03 Speech at the Urania Berlin*, p 23.

integration process."[286] The biggest obstacle for the Constitution is not the importance of national interests but rather the universal indifference among the electorate.[287]

3.3. Intermediate Conclusion

Concluding Part III, it seems that the final agreement became possible due to several (co-)incidents, well executed diplomacy and a wise Irish Presidency. Unfortunately, the outcome could not fully heal the wounds suffered from the previous failure and tough negotiations. The ratification should be, among a vote in the national parliaments, subjected to a European Referendum as described afore.

---

[286] B. Kaufmann, "Five Spanish lessons for Europe", http://euobserver.com/?aid=18459&sid=7, on Web 21 February 2005.
[287] S. Ulrich, "Europa in müder Verfassung", http://www.sueddeutsche.de/ausland/artikel/226/ 48178/print.html, on Web 22 February 2005.

PART IV

CONCLUDING REMARKS

Part IV
Concluding Remarks

As this paper makes plain to see the Constitution for Europe is a great opportunity for the European Union to be re-united in its diversity, provided with an unprecedent legal document and ready to cope with 25 members. However, the difficult process towards a common European constitution, though already being on the home stretch, may easily result in a setback, a EU of two or more speeds, if the document will not be ratified: A constitution meant to unite a Union of 25 countries could end up dividing it.

Non-ratification would be the omission of a unique historical, political and legal step for a whole continent, its 25 Member States and more than 450 million citizens. It is true that the constitution may not be ideal but it is the one which will allow us Europeans to proceed together and provide the EU with a firm foundation, legitimacy and a solid perspective in a globalized world.[288] Ratification of the Constitution would breathe new life into the Union as a whole, it would grant the EU a moment of necessary impetus and help its citizens as well as its leaders to realize the potential of the entity.

> The text may be complex, unreadable in places, and flabby with compromise [in some areas], but as a democratic undertaking by

---

[288] Cf. E. Teufel, Prime Minister of Baden-Württemberg in Germany, in his speech on the European Constitutional Treaty in the German Parliament on 24 February 2005.

25 sovereign states it is a substantial achievement, and proof an enlarged EU is not condemned to paralysis.[289]

Only a strong and unite Europe can tackle todays supra-national challenges like jobs, health, savings, terrorism, drugs, crime or economy. A codified and formally constitutionalised EU clarifies the current patchwork of Treaties, doctrines and jurisprudence. It encourages the further and clearer development of a common European identity or *demos* which will be complementary to the current national identities.

Also, citizens will be, for the first time ever, guaranteed fundamental rights by a common constitutional EU legal document in an area stretching from Portugal in the west to Latvia in the east and from Finland in the north to Greece in the far south. Moreover, the Constitutional Treaty is a success in the light of the objectives of the Declarations of Nice and Laeken, enhances transparency, legitimacy and effectiveness, simplifies the Union in several aspects and reorganizes it in a distinct manner. It is a huge advance on the current Treaty system. Decision-making would finally be subject to qualified majority voting and no longer be at risk to be blocked by a single state due to the principle of unanimity. Also, the Union's competences would be clearly allocated and the principle of subsidiarity has become flesh on the bones by the involvement of national parliament in the legislative procedure.

As the European Union is growing-up its legal framework should not be bypassed and suffer a setback. Denial of ratification

---

[289] G. Parker in the *Financial Times* as cited by K. Chhor in the *Western Press Review*, http://truthnews.com/month/2004060100.htm, on Web June 2004.

could possibly ruin more than half a century's work and the vision of a free, united and prosperous Europe. The EU would lose enormous influence on the level of world politics, its citizens would turn their backs on the Union which would consequently be deprived of its hard-won legitimacy.

As this confirms, there is no other way for the EU and its citizens than to ratify the Constitutional Treaty so that it will enter into force on 1 November 2006.

Thus, when finally ratified, the Constitution **will** be a point of no return – no return to the confusing, paralysing and unconvincing days of pillars, amalgam of Treaties, jurisprudence and doctrines, and legal uncertainty. In order to achieve this promising goal politicians and citizens alike might heed a piece of advice:

> Ask not what Europe can do for you and your country, but what your country [and you] can do for Europe.[290]

With the Constitutional Treaty after the signing on 29 October 2004 being ready for ratification the EU is at the crossroads - hopefully it will not decide to turn into the blind alley. The Member States should follow the 'European example' set by Hungary, Italy, Lithunia Slovenia and Spain who were the first countries to give a loud and clear 'yes' to Europe by crossing their national points of no return.

---

[290] Appeal of the Belgium Prime Minister Guy Verhofstadt in his speech "The new European Constitution from Laeken to Rome" on 25 November 2003, *Humboldt-Reden zu Europa Speech at the Humboldt-University Berlin*, p 12 f.

APPENDICES

Appendix 1

The History of the European Union

Year	Step of European Integration
After WW II	According to a concept developed by the French Jean Monnet the French Minister of Foreign Affairs, Robert Schuman, formed following plan: Germany's important resources for wartime economy, i.e. coal and steel, should be internationally supervised. However, this supervision should, contrary to the aftermath of WW I and the Treaty of Versaille, be founded on bilateralism and a supranational system.
1952	Foundation of the European Coal and Steel Community (ECSC) by a multilateral Treaty between six countries – Belgium, France, the Federal Republic of Germany, Italy, Luxembourg and the Netherlands – which was limited to 50 years.
1954	Attempt to found a European Defence Community foiled by veto of the French Parliament.
1958	The Rome Treaties entered into force and formed the European Economic Community (EEC) and the European Atomic Energy Community (EURATOM) between the six Member States of the ECSC.

Year	Step of European Integration
1967	The Merger Treaty of 8 April 1965 united the seperately existing organs of the three European Communities to a single Council and a single Commission.
1973	First enlargement of the European Community (EC) by the acession of Denmark, Ireland and the United Kingdom.
1979	First general elections to the European Parliament.
1981	Greece joins the EC on 1 January 1981
1986	Portugal and Spain become the 11th and 12th Member States of the EC on 1 January 1986.
1987	The Single European Act (SEA) enters into force on 1 July 1987 aiming to boost the realization of the Single European Market, introducing majority voting in that area of legislation and increasing powers of the European Parliament (EP).
1989	Collapse of the German Democratic Republic and fall of the Berlin Wall on 09 November 1989; Plan for the achievement of the European Monetary Union (EMU) is launched by the Madrid European Council
1990	Unification of East and West Germany on 3 October 1990

Year	Step of European Integration
1992	Signing of the Treaty on the European Union ("Maastricht Treaty") on 7 February 1992 at the European Council in Maastricht (NL).
1993	The Single Market enters into force on 1 January 1993.
1995	Austria, Finland and Sweden join the EU on 1 January 1995. The Norwegian people in a referendum reject to join the EU.
1999	The Euro is introduced as an official, though merely secondary, currency parallel to the existing national currencies in the EU. The Amsterdam Treaty enters into force on 1 May 1999.
2000	IGC of Nice agrees on a new Treaty.
2001	The IGC issues the "Declaration on the Future of Europe" (Laeken Declaration).
2002	The Euro becomes the official and sole currency for twelve Member States of the EU except Denmark, Sweden and the UK on 1 January 2002.

Year	Step of European Integration
2003	The Treaty of Nice enters into force on 1 February 2003. The Convention on the Future of Europe presents a "Draft Treaty establishing a Constitution for Europe" to the European Council in Thessaloniki (GRE) on 20 June 2003 and submits a final version on 18 July 2003. The IGC of Brussels in December fails to agree on the Draft Treaty.
2004	On 1 May 2004 ten countries join the EU in its biggest enlargement, raising the number of Member States to 25: Cyprus, Czech Republic, Estonia, Hungary, Latvia, Lithunia, Malta, Poland, Slovak Republic and Slovenia. On 19 June 2004 the European Council agrees on a revised version of the Draft Constitution proposed by the Convention. Signed on 29 October 2004 and shall, after ratification by all Member States, enter into force on 01 November 2006. Ratification by Hungarian and Lithunian Parliaments in late 2004.
2005	Ratification of the Constitution by the Slovenian Parliament on 01 February 2005 and the Italian Parliament. The first referendum took place in Spain on 20 February 2005. The vast majority of the votes was in favour of the Constitutional Treaty.

Appendix 2

National v European Identity*

Member State	Nationality only in %	Some European Element in Identity in %
Austria	50	47
Belgium	39	59
Cyprus	51	48
Czech Republic	49	49
Denmark	43	56
Estonia	44	55
Finland	60	40
France	29	68
Germany	38	60
Greece	55	44
Hungary	62	37
Ireland	49	49
Italy	28	67
Latvia	38	52
Lithunia	54	41
Luxembourg	27	69
Malta	37	61
Netherlands	48	50
Poland	45	54
Portugal	46	53
Slovak Republic	36	62
Slovenia	41	57
Spain	32	65

Member State	Nationality only in %	Some European Element in Identity in %
Sweden	57	41
UK	62	35
EU-25	41	56

* Opinion Poll by Eurobarometer (Flash EB 159), May 2004, "In the near future, do you see yourself as national only OR national with some European identity?"

Appendix 3

Main Reforms to the Institutional Framework

Institution	Reforms & Provisions	From when
European Council	becomes an institution, Arts I-19 (1), I-21 will be chaired by a permanent President for 2 ½ years, Art. I-22 (1)	Entry into force of the Constitution
EU Minister of Foreign Affairs	merges the tasks of the High Representative for the CFSP and the External Relations Commissioner, Art. I-28 (2), (4) will be a member of the Commission, Art. I-28 (4) will get his / her mandate from the Council for CFSP, Art. I-28 (2) will chair the External Relations Council, Art. I-28 (4)	Entry into force of the Constitution

Institution	Reform & Provisions	From when
Council of Ministers	Presidency of the different Council formations will rotate on 6-month basis unless meeting as External Relations Council, Art. I-24 (7) System may be altered by European Council by qualified majority, Art. I-24 (4)	Entry into force of the Constitution
European Parliament	increased powers: 95% of European laws will be adopted under the co-decision procedure ("ordinary legislative decision"), Arts I-20 (1), I-34 (1), III-396 maximum number of seats is raised to 750, Art. I-20 (2) minimum / maximum number of seats per Member State: 6 / 96, Art. I-20 (2)	Decision proposed by the EP and adopted unani-mously by European Council on EP's composition before the European elections 2009

Institution	Reform & Provisions	From when
Commission	one Commissioner per Member State principle maintained until 2014, Art. I-26 (5)	
	from 2014 the number of Commissioners will be reduced to 2/3 of the number of Member States (incl. both its President and the EU Minister for Foreign Affairs), Art. I-26 (6)	
	the Commissioners will be chosen on the basis of equal rotation among the Member States, Art. I-26 (6)	November 2014
	the Commission (incl. both the President and the Minister for Foreign Affairs) has to be approved by the European Parliament before being appointed by the European Council, Art. I-27 (2)	

Appendix 4

Press Reviews

I. Following all by Khatya Chhor, Radio Free Europe/Radio Liberty:

THE WASHINGTON TIMES - USA
(editorial)

"The problem with the European Union is that Europeans have yet to feel unified. [... the results of the 13 June European Parliament elections] suggests that enthusiasm and influence have switched to Eurosceptic parties [which won plurality in the parliament ...] dreams of EU elites to fashion a European superstate in the mold of the United States appear as far away as ever. [... If] voters in EU member states decide their welfare would be improved by relinquishing much of their national sovereignty, so be it. [...But las week's poll indicates something else] Not only did Eurosceptic parties gain the upper hand in the parliament, but voter turnout reached its lowest level since direct elections were instituted in 1979. [Smaller states are rightly concerned that ultimately, EU power will remain in a] Paris-Berlin-Brussels axis. [Last week's struggle to agree on a European constitution underscored the difficulties of reaching agreement in the new Europe of 25 member states. At] 200 pages and counting, the EU constitution is more an exercise in piddling legalities than in promoting the public welfare. While debating constitutional minutiae, European leaders should not ignore the fact that many Europeans simply do not understand how a superstate will benefit them, nor do they care very much. [...] Plowing ahead with fantasies of a continent united while ignoring national sovereignty [will] lead to failure."

FINANCIAL TIMES - USA
(George Parker)

"[The hard-won agreement on a EU constitution, reached early one morning] discarded champagne bottles [and] exhausted officials [was the Irish Prime Minister Bertie Ahern's] greatest political triumph. [...] The EU needs these moments of euphoria and historical hyperbole, those rare occasions when one can glimpse the sunlit peaks of European ambition through the fog of national rivalries and bureaucratic wrangling. [But this does] not mark the end of the story for Europe's new constitution. Long after the detritus [is] cleared away, the question remains whether the constitution can make an enlarged Europe work. A second question is whether it will ever come into force. [The text now has to be ratified in all 25 member states, and many will hold national referenda on the issue.]. It is clear that two years of hard political slog lie ahead. [But in fact, the new EU document is not really a constitution, which is normally thought of as a contract between the government and the governed. It is more of a constitutional treaty, an agreement between 25 sovereign states. It is] a dense text, with simplicity sacrificed on the altar of political compromise. [The constitutional treaty] may be complex, unreadable in places, and flabby with compromise, but as a democratic undertaking by 25 sovereign states it is a substantial achievement, and proof an enlarged EU is not condemned to paralysis."

LE MONDE - FRA
(editorial)

"[The Agreement on a new EU constitution is] good news for Europe. The new text is historical, and likely to reinforce the European Union's coherence and its place in the world. But this advance cannot eclipse the failure of the 25 member states to agree on appointing a new president of the European Commission. This shortcoming tarnishes the success of the constitutional treaty and confirms the deep and lasting differences that persist within the EU. The union of 25 is majorly divided, and its capacity for action is thus seriously curtailed. The effectiveness of the constitution remains uncertain for three main reasons. First, because it is still subject to being approved by national referenda. And judging by the apathy and Euro-scepticism of the 13 June EU parliamentary elections across Europe, winning this approval will be no easy matter. Secondly, the divisions that became apparent over the lengthy negotiations on the constitutional text have left some grasping gaps. Finally, in many aspects, the spirit of unity is generally on the decline in the European Union, which must now redefine its ambitions as a result. These lasting divides are the principle cause of Europe's weakness. [...] The reform introduced by the constitutional treaty are far from negligible, however, and will ultimately make the EU more effective. But without the strong political will to overcome the divergences between member states, the new constitution, whatever its virtues, will not be enough."

THE INDEPENDENT - UK
(Bruce Anderson)

"[...The European Union would like to have emerged from its weekend negotiations convincing the world that the new EU constitutional treaty is a triumph. But there] is one fundamental objection to the new document [...] It is an outdated solution to the wrong problem. [Of course Europe needs rules ... and with enlargement] new and clear procedures were necessary to ensure that Europe would run efficiently. [But the new constitution] has nothing to do with any of [that]. There is nothing in it that would end the decade-long scandal of the EU's own court of auditors being unable to sign accounts because fraud and large-scale financial evaporation. [The new constitution also] gives the

EU vague but extensive new powers over economic matters, social policy, criminal justice and defense. [And it is reasonably certain] that the EU's institutions would be further strengthened, at Britain's expense. [...] Every time we have signed up to a European treaty, we have found ourselves committed to far more than we had expected. [The European Union] needed a loose regulatory framework for the single market. Within that broad structure there would be nothing to prevent individual states from negotiating bilateral or multilateral arrangements to pool sovereignty. [Instead ... Europe now has a text that is] an attempt at coercion that is bound to founder on the rocks of popular will [when it is put to a referendum by member states].

LE FIGARO - FRA
(Pierre Rouslin)

"[T]he inability to agree on a new European Commission president to replace the outgoing Romano Prodi is a real pity, since one could have hoped that the agreement on an EU constitution would have breathed new life into the union as a whole. At a crucial moment in the history of the European Union, no one has come forward to lead the EU executive branch. This is a distressing point [...]. But let us recognize that perhaps this is not an enviable post [...]. Following the enlargement to 25 members, cacophony and chaos loom. Paris and Berlin agreed to back Belgian Prime Minister Guy Verhofstadt – but apparently, because he was the Fraco-German choice; London had to disagree. The old divisions over the war in Iraq also emerged, once again dividing the continent into 'Old Europe' and 'New Europe', just when all hoped this gap had been bridged. [... I]t is time to stop refighting the battles of last year and concentrate instead on the EU's shared future.

II. Following all by Richard Carter, http://www.euobserver.com

THE GUARDIAN - UK

"Mr Blair is right to make the case in an unapologetic tone. He needs to continue to do so and to be supported by others of all parties – including any Tories still professing to be in favour of UK membership of the EU ... This is truly a defining national moment."

THE SUN - UK

"Blair faces a massive wave of protest today from all sides, over his arrogance in pushing Britain where it does not want to go."

LE MONDE - FRA

"The adoption of the European Constitutional project by 25 Heads of EU governments is good news for Europe ... Europe needs to give itself a way of functioning with 25 members, soon to be 27 ... we should therefore be pleased that this has finally happened, even if it was not achieved without some pain."

ASAHI SHIMBUN – Japan

"The fact the individual countries have shared the common goal of steadily pushing toward integration, regardless of how many years may be required, has clearly helped strengthen European progress and drive ... Over half a century has passed since the first cautious steps by Europe in this direction. With the breakthrough agreement on the bloc's first constitution, the countries there appear to have at last arrived at a true milestone in the long and hard road to unification."

LA LIBRE BELGIQUE – Belgium

"While the Constitution itself was finalised yesterday evening around 11 pm, with the consensus reached by the heads of the state and government, it will not necessarily enter into force. Because the leaders have not foreseen anything to implement it in the countries which will ratify it, if one [other EU country's] parliament or a population decides to reject it. The referendum bomb is ticking ..."

THE ECONOMIST – UK

"Europe's leaders might fairly congratulate themselves, since many thought no agreement was possible on Friday night, they toasted with champagne. But after their celebration will come a hangover of bitterness over the rows at the summit. And hangover or no, the EU's leaders must now go straight to work selling Europe's more sceptical electorates on the virtues of their new constitution."

NCR HANDELSBLAD – NL

"'Europe has a constitution for the first time during its existence', said the Belgian Prime Minister Verhofstadt yesterday night. But with a minimum of seven referenda in different EU countries to be expected – each of them being able to block the Constitution in the whole EU – that remains to be seen."

SÜDDEUTSCHE ZEITUNG – GER

"The negotiations at the Brussel Summit raise doubts as to whether the EU is really capable of profiting from this Constitution. Many of the 25 governments were not mainly concerned to make the EU more capable of decision-making, but rather to block decisions as easily as possible. This is how the bloc of blockers succeeded in damaging the Draft Constitution in several fields, in favour of national egoisms."

DER TAGESSPIEGEL – GER

"One of the most grave misunderstandings can be seen in the proud feelings over the common EU Foreign Minister – that the EU could overcome substantial divergences of opinion if it only introduces new institutions. The 25 EU states and especially the big six (Germany, France, the UK, Italy, Spain and Poland) each have their own foreign policy interests, for good reasons. A common EU Foreign Minister will not be able to bridge these divides either."

III. Following all on http://www.newsvote.bbc.co.uk

LE FIGARO – FRA

"Paris and Berlin wanted qualified majority voting to be extended to taxation and social security system. Sticking to his right of veto, Tony Blair said 'no', closing the door on any harmonisation in these areas ... Blair is playing his cards right. Ever since he announced that the constitution would be put to a referendum in his country, he has had a very good reason to be inflexible in Brussels. This is one of the great paradoxes of the EU: its most sceptical member has the upper hand."

LE SOIR – Belgium
(Editorial)

"So as not to ruin the political career of Europhile Blair, so as not to sacrifice someone who is still an objective ally, the most determined European federalists had no choice but to back down"

LA LIBRE BELGIQUE – Belgium
("Message to Tony Blair")

"Why did you join the Union, other than to sabotage it ? Not only have you twice objected to a Belgian candidate as president of the European Commission, but you have also been fighting hard at the Brussels summit to erode a constitution which represents a real advance for 450 million Europeans. However, one thing is certain: Europe needs ambition, not just pragmatism. You need to tell this to your electorate. Good luck with your referendum."

LIBERATION – FRA
(Editorial)

"After the storm of the European Parliament elections, the leaders of the Union needed to show they were determined to strengthen the ship on which the European have set sailed. They did so on Friday by adopting the first European Constitution, but not without first presenting the sorry sight of a mutinous crew, unable to agree on the name of the captain, squabbling over whose hand should be on the tiller, and with no idea about which direction to head."

ABC –ESP
(Editorial)

"Europe reached an historic milestone yesterday ... nevertheless, the almost 300 pages of the finalised constitution, without being the gibberish of Nice [Treaty], reflect a complex Union plagued by reservations, revocations, 'emergency brakes' and 'red lines'."

EL PAÍS – ESP
(Report)

"Last night Europe made the greatest leap in its history towards political union when it gave birth to a first constitution for 455m inhabitants in 25 different countries ... the 25 heads of states and government last night approved, what is set to be the constitution of the entire continent."

(Editorial)

"[This] is not a constitution in the proper sense of the world, as the EU is not a state, and the unanimous ratification by 25 signatory states is still required, something which at the moment does not even seem likely."

EL MUNDO – ESP
(Editorial)

"Only a fool would dare deny that the agreement reached yesterday in Brussels means a loss of power for Spain with respect to the Nice Treaty ... The agreement reached yesterday is, on the other hand, not as bad as we could reasonably have feared."

IL CORRIERE DELLA SERA – ITA
(Editorial)

"The British succeeded once again in slowing down and diluting the process of integration ... There are at least two families in Europe inspired by different philosophies. Logic would require that their differences should be recognised and that they should each be able to follow their own path."

TRYBUNA – POL

"It has probably not completely sunk in, and not to everyone, that Brussels is not a game to play on a computer but one of competing interests. We want to have the greatest possible influence on the decisions made there, but this does not depend on Polish possibilities and abilities. Even if you correctly work out when you can be tough and decisive and when you should turn down the volume a bit. Apart from Poland, there are two dozen states larger and smaller than we are. To achieve a compromise capable of being accepted by everyone, although not fully satisfying everyone, is not easy."

THE IRISH TIMES – IRE
(Editorial)

"It is an historic and unprecedent foundational text for this new political entity on the world stage ... It is an honourable compromise between contrasting views of voting, representation and economic governance, based on intense consultation and a shrewd judgment about what would be acceptable to Ireland's EU partners. It deserves the most careful attention of EU citizens as they decide whether to ratify it over the next two years."

PUBLICO – POR
(Commentary)

"The constitution that the leaders approved yesterday may not be ideal; however, as always in the Union, it is the one that will allow us to proceed together and provide Europe with the minimum of institutional and political foundations ... an important hurdle has been cleared."

Appendix 5

Referenda in the EU

Member State	Referendum?	Status quo	Public opinion on Constitution*	Possible Concern
Austria	No	May 2005 by Parliament	Pro: 68 % Contra: 23 %	
Belgium	Yes	2005 by Parliament	Pro: 85 % Contra: 10 %	
Cyprus	No	March 2005 by Parliament	Pro: 80 % Contra: 11 %	
Czech Republic	Yes	June 2006	Pro: 64 % Contra: 17 %	Concern that Constitution handicaps smaller Member States
Denmark	Yes	27 September 2005	Pro: 60 % Contra: 29 %	Loss of sovereignty; rise of federal superstate
Estonia	Unlikely	Discussion in Parliament and media; no date scheduled	Pro: 60 % Contra: 10 %	
Finland	No	Decision by PM M. Vanhanen on 15 August 2004; end of 2005 or 2006	Pro: 68 % Contra: 20 %	

Member State	Referendum?	Status quo	Public opinion on Constitution*	Possible Concerns
France	Yes	Announced by President Chirac on 14 July 2004; May / 29 May 2005	Pro: 81 % Contra: 14 %	EU seen pushing freemarket policies; French language losing influence, sovereignty
Germany	No	Chancellor Schröder prefers European referendum; parliamentary procedure launched, adoption envisaged for 12 May 2005	Pro: 83 % Contra: 14 %	
Greece	No	Expected before June 2005	Pro: 89 % Contra: 9 %	
Hungary	No	Ratified on 20 December 2004	Pro: 87 % Contra: 5 %	
Ireland	Yes	Tradition referenda on EU issues; end of 2005; also parliamentary procedure	Pro: 80 % Contra: 11 %	

Member State	Referendum?	Status quo	Public opinion on Constitution*	Possible Concerns
Italy	No	Chamber, 25/1, and Senate, 6/4, ratified CT	Pro: 92 % Contra: 7 %	Lack of reference to christianity; sovereignty
Latvia	No	2005	Pro: 66 % Contra: 11 %	
Lithunia	No	Ratified by Parliament on 11 November 2004	Pro: 81 % Contra: 9 %	
Luxembourg	Yes (consultative)	Referendum takes place on 10 July 2005	Pro: 86 % Contra: 11 %	Some concern that Constitution handicaps smaller Member States
Malta	No	PM Fenech ruled out option referendum on 17 October 2003; July 2005	Pro: 61 % Contra: 15 %	
Netherlands	Yes (consultative)	1 June 2005	Pro: 70 % Contra: 21 %	
Poland	Yes	Autumn 2005	Pro: 72 % Contra: 18 %	Lost voting power due to Double Majority System

Member State	Referendum?	Status quo	Public opinion on Constitution*	Possible Concerns
Portugal	Yes	Announced by former PM and President of the Commission Barroso on 23 June 2004; autumn 2005	Pro: 81 % Contra: 10 %	Concern that Constitution handicaps smaller Member States
Slovak Rep.	Unlikely	Ratification by Parliament in May 2005	Pro: 70 % Contra: 13 %	Lack of reference to Christianity
Slovenia	No	Parliament ratified on 01 February 2005	Pro: 86 % Contra: 5 %	
Spain	Yes (consultative)	20 February 2005: Pro: 76,7 % Contra: 17 % Also ratification by parliament later in 2005	Pro: 85 % Contra: 7 %	Lost voting power due to Double Majority System
Sweden	No	Referenda only when there are splits within the parties; December 2005	Pro: 58 % Contra: 26 %	

Member State	Referendum?	Status quo	Public opinion on Constitution*	Possible Concerns
U.K.	Yes (consultative)	Announced by PM Blair on 20 April 2004; probably 2006	Pro: 51 % Contra: 30 %	Loss of sovereignty; rise of federal superstate

* Opinion Poll by Eurobarometer (Flash EB 159), May 2004, "Should the European Union adopt a Constitution ?"

Bibliography

I. Main Sources

Treaty establishing a Constitution for Europe [CIG 87/04 including Addendum 1 (Protocols) and 2 (Declarations), 6 August 2004], published in the Official Journal of the EU, C-310, Vol. 47 December 2004, 1-474

The Laeken Declaration, 15 December 2001

Nice Treaty Declaration No 23, 26 February 2001

II. Further Sources

(i) Legal Provisions

Grundgesetz der Bundesrepublik Deutschland

Protocol Amending the EURATOM Treaty

Protocol on the application of the principles of subsidiarity and proportionality (provisional consolidated version of the Protocols annexed to the Treaty establishing a Constitution for Europe and of Annexes I and II, Addendum 1 to CIG 87/04)

Protocol on the Enlargement of the European Union (Protocol added to the Treaty of Nice)

Protocol on the role of Member States' national Parliaments in the European Union (provisional consolidated version of the Protocols annexed to the Treaty establishing a Constitution for Europe and of Annexes I and II, Addendum 1 to CIG 87/04)

The Treaty on European Union (consolidated version after the Treaty of Nice)

Treaty Establishing the European Community (consolidated version established after the Treaty of Nice)

Vienna Convention on the Law of Treaties

(ii) Cases

<u>(a) European Court of Justice</u>

Case 26/62 *NV Algemene Transport- en Expeditie Onderneming van Gend en Loos v Nederlandse Administratie der Belastingen* [1963] ECR 1

Case 6/64 *Flaminio Costa v Ente Nazionale per l'Energia Elletrica (ENEL)* [1964] ECR 585

Case 11/70 *Internationale Handelsgesellschaft mbH v Einfuhr- und Vorratsstelle für Getreide und Futtermittel* [1970] ECR 1125

Case 41/74 *Van Duyn v Home Office* [1974] ECR 1337

Case 106/77 *Amministrazione delle Finanze dello Stato v Simmenthal SpA* [1978] ECR 629

Case 149/77 *Defrenne v SABENA* [1979] ECR 1365

Case 294/83 *Partie écologiste 'Les Verts' v European Parliament* [1986] ECR 1339

Case C-213/89, *Factortame Ltd v Secretary of State for Transport (No. 2)* [1990] ECR I-2243

C-6 and C-9/90 *Andrea Francovich and Others v Italian Republic* [1991] ECR I-5357

Opinion 1/91 [1991] ECR I-6079

Case C-314/91 *Beate Weber v European Parliament* [1993] ECR I-1093

C-46 and C-48/93 *Brasserie du Pêcheur SA v Germany (Factortame No. 3)* [1996] ECR I-1029

C-224/01 *Gerhard Köbler v Republik Österreich* [2003], not yet published in the ECR

(b) Other Courts

German *Bundesverfassungsgericht*:
Cases 2 BvR 2134/92 & 2159/92 *Maastricht*, 89 BVerfGE 155; reported in English as *Manfred Brunner v The European Union Treaty* [1994] 1 Common Market Law Review (C.M.L.Rev.) 57

(iii) Commission

White Paper on Governance (COM 2001 / 428)

(iv) Council of the European Union

Presidency Conclusion, Addendum to the Cover Note of the Brussels European Council (10679/04)

(v) Books

BROWN, L. Neville and KENNEDY, Tom, *The Court of Justice of the European Communities* (5th ed), London: Sweet & Maxwell, 2000

CRAIG, Paul and DE BÚRCA, Gráinne, *EU Law*, Oxford, Oxford University Press, 2002

CRAIG, Paul and DE BÚRCA, Gráinne (eds), *The Evolution of EU Law*, Oxford, Oxford University Press, 1999

DE SMITH, Stanley and BRAZIER, Rodney, *Constitutional and Administrative Law* (8th ed), London: Penguin Books, 1990

DOUGLAS-SCOTT, Sionaidh, *Constitutional Law of the European Union* Harlow, England - London *et al.*: Pearson Education, 2002

GARNER, Bryan A. (ed), *Black's Law Dictionary* (7th ed.) St. Paul, Minnesota: West Group, 1999

HARTLEY, Trevor C., *The Foundations of European Community Law: An Introduction to the constitutional and administrative law of the European Community* (5th ed.) Oxford: Oxford University Press, 2003

HARTLEY, Trevor C., *Constitutional Problems of the European Union*, Oxford – Portland - Oregon: Hart Publishing, 1999

HOBSBAWM, Eric J., *Nations and Nationalism since 1780: Programm, Myth, Reality*, Cambridge: Cambridge University Press, 1992

MacCORMICK, Neil, *A Union of its Own Kind ? Reflections on the European Convention and the proposed Constitution of the European Union*, Edinburgh, 2004

MADURO, Miguel Poiares, *We the Court: The European Court of Justice and the European Economic Constitution*, Oxford: Hart Publishing, 1997

MARTIN, Elizabeth A. (ed), *A Dictionary of Law* (4th ed) Oxford: Oxford University Press, 1997

PENNER, James E., *Mozley & Whiteley's Law Dictionary* (12th ed) London – Edinburgh – Dublin: Butterworths, 2001

RASMUSSEN, Hjalte, *The European Court of Justice*, Copenhagen: GadJura Publishers, 1998

THOMPSON, Brian, *Textbook on Constitutional and Administrative Law* (3rd ed.) London: Blackstone Press Limited, 1998

WEILER, Joseph H. H., *The constitution of Europe: 'Do the new clothes have an emperor?' and other essays on European integration*, Cambridge: Cambridge University Press, 1999

(vi) **Articles**

ARNULL, Anthony / CHALMERS, Damian, "Editorial: A Constitution whose bottle is definitely half-full and not half-empty", (2003) *28 E.L.Rev.* 449-450

BERMANN, George A., "Editorial: The European Union as a Constitutional Experiment", (2004) *10 European Law Journal (E.L.J.)* 363-370

BRAND, Michiel, "Affirming and Refining European Constitutionalism: Towards the Establishment of the First Constitution for the European Union", (2004) European University Institut Florence *EUI Working Paper LAW No. 2004/2*, 1-58

BREUER, Marten, "State liability for judicial wrongs and Community law: the case of *Gerhard Köbler v Austria*", (2004) *29 European Law Review (E.L.Rev.)* 243-254

CHALMERS, Damian "Editorial: The European transformation of national government", (2004) *29 European Law Review (E.L.Rev.)* 151-152

COMMISSION, "Summary of the agreement on the Constitutional Treaty", URL http://europa.eu.int/futurum, on Web June 2004

COUNCIL OF THE EUROPEAN UNION, "Presidency Conclusions – Brussels, Addendum 1" (2004)

CRAIG, Paul, "Constitutions, Constitutionalism and the European Union", (2001) 7 *European Law Journal (E.L.J.)* 125-150

DAVIES, Gareth, "The post-Laeken division of powers", (2003) *28 European Law Review (E.L.Rev.)* 686-698

DE BÚRCA, Gráinne and DE WITTE, Bruno, "The Delimitation of Powers Between the EU and its Member States" in A. Arnull and D. Wincott (eds), *Accountability and Legitimacy in the European Union* (Oxford, Oxford University Press, 2002), 201-222

DE BÚRCA, Gráinne, "Setting Constitutional Limits to EU Competence?", (2001) Francisco Lucas Pires Working Papers Series on European Constitutionalism, Working Paper 2001/02

DE BÚRCA, Gráinne, "The constitutional challenge of new governance in the European Union", (2003) *28 European Law Review (E.L.Rev.)* 814-839

DE WITTE, Bruno, "Direct Effect, Supremacy, and the Nature of the Legal Order", in P. Craig and G. de Búrca (eds), *The Evolution of EU law* (Oxford: Oxford University Press, 1999), 177-213

DI FABIO, Udo, "Some Remarks on the Allocation of Competences between the EU and its Member States", (2002) *39 Common Market Law Review (C.M.L.Rev.)* 1289-1302

DI FABIO, Udo, "The European Constitutional Treaty: An Analysis", (2004) 5 *German Law Journal No. 8 August (G.L.J.)*, URL http://www.germanlawjournal.com, on Web August 2004

DORAU, Christoph and JACOBI, Philipp, "The Debate over a 'European Constitution': Is it Solely a German Concern ?", (2000) 6 *European Public Law (E.P.L.)* 413-428

DOUGAN, Michael, "The Convention's Draft Constitutional Treaty: A 'Tidying-Up Exercise' that Needs Some Tidying-Up of Its Own", (2003) *Online Paper 27/03 The Federal Trust for Education nd Research*, 1-18

DOUGAN, Michael, "The Convention's Draft Constitutional Treaty: bringing Europe closer to its lawyers ?", (2003) *28 European Law Review (E.L.Rev.)* 763-794

DUTHEIL DE LA ROCHÈRE, Jaqueline and PERNICE, Ingolf, "European Union Law and National Constitutions", in M. Andenas and J. A. Usher (eds), *The Treaty of Nice and beyond: Enlargement and Constitutional Reform* (Oxford-Portland, Oregon: Hart Publishing, 2003), 47-105

DZURINDA, Mikulás, "The Debate on the European Constitution – a Slovak View", (2002) *Forum Constitutionis Europae FCE Spezial 1/02* 2-8

EDWARD, David, "Judicial Activism – Myth or Reality ? *Van Gend en Loos*, *Costa v ENEL* and the *Van Duyn* family revisited", in A. Campbell and Voyatzi (eds), *Legal reasoning and Judicial Interpretation of European Law* (Trenton, 1996), 29-67

ELEFTHERIADIS, Pavlos, "Constitution or Treaty ?", (2004) *Online Paper 12/04* URL http://www.fedtrust.co.uk, 1-12, on Web August 2004

GERSTENBERG, Oliver, "Expanding the Constitution beyond the Court:The Case of Euro-Constitutionalism", (2002) 8 *European Law Journal (E.L.J.)* 172-192

GORING, Randi L., "Requirements for the Emerging European Constitution", (2002) *Walter Hallstein-Institut Humboldt-University of Berlin WHI-Paper 2/03* 2-15.

GRIMM, Dieter "Does Europe need a Constitution ?", (1995) *1 European Law Journal (E.L.J.)* 282-302

HABERMAS, Jürgen, "Why Europe needs a Constitution", (2001) *11 New Left Review* (16 pages), URL http://www.newleftreview.net/NLR24501.shtml, on Web July 2004

HÄNSCH, Klaus, "Der Verfassungsentwurf für die Europäische Union nach der Regierungskonferenz", (2004) *Forum Constitutionis Europae FCE 2/04* 2-8

HOBE, Stephan, "Bedingungen, Verfahren und Chancen europäischer Verfassungsgebung", (2003) *38 Europarecht* 1-16

HUGHES, Kirsty, "A new division of power in the EU ?", (2004) *EU Constitution Project Newsletter Special Issue July* (The Federal Trust for Education and Research) 1-16

ISENSEE, Josef, "Staat und Verfassung", in J. Isensee and P. Kirchhof (eds), *Handbuch des Staatsrechts Bd. 1* (1987), Chapter § 13

JACKSON, John H., "Status of Treaties in Domestic Legal Systems: A Policy Analysis", (1992) *86 American Law Journal of International Law* 310-340

KOKOTT, Juliane and RÜTH, Alexandra, "The European Convention and its Draft Treaty establishing a Constitution for Europe: Appropriate answers to the Laeken questions?", (2003) *40 Common Market Law Review (C.M.L.Rev.)* 1315-1345

LENAERTS, Koen and DESOMER, Marlies, "Bricks for a Constitutional Treaty", (2002) *27 European Law Review (E.L.Rev.)* 377-407

LENAERTS, Koen and GERARD, Damien, "The structure of the Union according to the Constitution for Europe: the emperor is getting dressed", (2004) *29 European Law Review (E.L.Rev.)* 289-322

MANCINI, Federico, "The Making of a Constitution for Europe", (1989) *26 Common Market Law Review (C.M.L.Rev.)* 595-614

MANCINI, Federico, "Europe: The Case for Statehood", (1998) *4 European Law Journal (E.L.J.)* 29-42

NETTESHEIM, Martin, "EU-Recht und nationales Verfassungsrecht: Deutscher Bericht", in Lord Slynn of Hadley and M. Andenas (eds), *FIDE XX. Congress London 2002, Volume 1, National Reports* (London: British Institute of International and Comparative Law, 2002), 81

PERNICE, Ingolf, "Die neue Verfassung der Europäischen Union – ein historischer Fortschritt zu einem Europäischen Bundesstaat ?", (2003) *Forum Constitutionis Europae FCE Spezial 1/03 Speech at the Urania Berlin*, 1-23

PERNICE, Ingolf, "Multilevel Constitution in the EU", (2002) *27 European Law Review (E.L.Rev.)* 511-529

PETERS, Anne, "European Democracy after the 2003 Convention", (2004) *41 Common Market Law Review (C.M.L.Rev.)* 37-85

PHINNEMORE, David, "And now the really difficult bit ... ratification", (2004) *EU Constitution Project Newsletter Special Issue July*, 14-15

PIEPENSCHNEIDER, Melanie, "Vertragsgrundlagen und Entscheidungsverfahren", (2003) *279 Informationen zur politischen Bildung* 17-26

PIRIS, Jean-Claude, "Does the European Union have a Constitution? Does it need one?", (1999) *24 European Law Review (E.L.Rev.)* 557-585

POLLICINO, Oreste, "Legal Reasoning of the Court of Justice in the Context of the Principle of Equality between Judicial Activism and Self-restraint", (2003) *German Law Journal Vol. 5 (G.L.J.)* 283-317

RASMUSSEN, Hjalte, "Between Self-restraint and Activism: A Judicial Policy for the European Court", (1996) *13 European Law Review (E.L.Rev.)* 28-38

RAZ, Joseph, "On the Authority and Interpretation of Constitutions: Some Preliminaries", in L. Alexander (ed.), *Constitutionalism: Philosophical foundations* (Cambridge, Cambridge University Press, 1998), 152-193

SCHMUCK, Otto, "Reformperspektiven und Verfassungsfragen", (2003) *279 Informationen zur politischen Bildung* 53-59

SCHUMAN, Robert, "Declaration of 9 May 1950", http://www.robert-schuman.org/anglais/robert-schuman/ declaration2.htm

SCHWARZE, Jürgen, "The Convention's Draft Treaty establishing a Constitution for Europe", (2003) *40 Common Market Law Review (C.M.L.Rev.)* 1037-1045

TEUFEL, Erwin, "Konturen der Europäischen Verfassung", (2003) *Forum Constitutionis Europae FCE 3/03* 1-12

THYM, Daniel, "European Constitutional Theory and the Post-Nice Process", in M. Andenas and J. A. Usher (eds), *The Treaty of Nice and Beyond: Enlargement and Constitutional Reform* (Oxford-Portland, Oregon: Hart Publishing, 2003), 147-180.

TRIDIMAS, Takis, "The Court of Justice and Judicial Activism", (1996) *21 European Law Review (E.L.Rev.)* 199-210

VERHOFSTADT, Guy, "The new European Constitution from Laeken to Rome", (2003) *Humboldt-Reden zu Europa*, http://www.rewi.hu-berlin.de/WHI/english/index.htm, on Web July 2004

WALKER, Neil, "After the Constitutional Moment", (2003) *Online Paper 32/03 The Federal Trust for Education and Research*, 1-15.

WALKER, Neil, "Constitutionalising Enlargement, Enlarging Constitutionalism", (2003) *28 European Law Review (E.L.Rev.)* 365-385.

WALKER, Neil, "European Constitutionalism and European Integration", (1996) *Public Law* 266-290

WALKER, Neil, "Postnational Constitutionalism and the Problem of Translation", (2003) *Working Paper IILJ 2003/03* (Institute for International Law and Justice, New York University), 1-36

WALKER, Neil, "The EU as a Constitutional Project", (2004) http://www.fedtrust.co.uk/default.asp?pageid=1878&mpageid=67&msubid=75&groupid=6, on Web July 2004

WALKER, Neil, "The Idea of Constitutional Pluralism", (2002) *65 Modern Law Review (M.L.Rev.)* 317-359

WEATHERILL, Stephen, "Is constitutional finality feasible or desirable? On the cases for European constitutionalism and a European Constitution", (2002) *Constitutionalism Web-Papers, ConWEB No. 7/2002*, URL http://les1.man.ac.uk/conweb/, on Web July 2004

WEILER, Joseph H. H., "Does Europe Need a Constitution ? Demos, Telos and the German Maastricht Decision", (1995) *European Law Journal (E.L.J.)* 219-258

WEILER, Joseph H. H., "Europe: The Case Against the Case for Statehood", (1998) *European Law Journal (E.L.J.)* 43-62

(vii) Others

ANDERSON, Bruce, "The European constitution remains an outdated solution to the wrong problem", *The Independent* 21 June 2004 p 25

BEATTY, Andrew, "Blair to expose 'EU myths'", URL http://euobserver.com /?aid=16684&sid=9, on Web July 2004

BEATTY, Andrew, "Blair to reaffirm Constitution 'red lines'", URL http://euobserver.com/?aid=15573&sid=9, on Web July 2004

BEATTY, Andrew, "Spains shows its hand in Constitution debate", URL http://euobserver.com/?aid=15597&sid=9, on Web July 2004

BEATTY, Andrew, "Madrid announces February referendum on Constitution", URL http://euobserver.com/?aid=16995&sid=18, on Web August 2004

BESTE, Ralf / FELDENKIRCHEN, Markus / HILDEBRANDT, Tina / KLOTH, Hans Michael / NELLES, Roland and PIEPER, Dietmar, "Furcht vor dem Volk", *31 Der Spiegel* 26 July 2004, p 22-26

BEUNDERMAN, Mark, "Dutch set to hold Constitution referendum this December", URL http://euobserver.com/?aid=16706&sid=9, on Web July 2004

BEUNDERMAN, Mark, "German referendum on EU may be legally possible", URL http://euobserver.com/?aid=17005&sid=18, on Web August 2004

CARTER, Richard, "Constitution: Press Review", URL http://www.euobserver.com, on Web June 2004

CARTER, Richard, "Finland to announce referendum 'in the coming weeks'", URL http://euobserver.com/?aid=16997&sid=18, on Web August 2004

CARTER, Richard, "Giscard calls for French referendum on Constitution", URL http://euobserver.com/?aid=15336&sid=9, on Web July 2004

CARTER, Richard, "Schröder: Constitution even without ratification", URL http://euobserver.com/?aid=15353&sid=9, on Web July 2004

CASTLE, Stephen, "Blair gives Chirac go-ahead for multi-speed union in exchange for veto", *The Independent on Sunday* 20 June 2004 p 20

CHHOR, Khatya, "Western Press Review", URL http://truthnews.com/month/2004060100.htm, on Web June 2004

DE GROOT, Gerhard, "Auch der Beichtstuhl half nicht mehr", *Kölner Stadt-Anzeiger* 15 December 2003 p 2

DIDZOLEIT, Winfried and KOCH, Dirk, "Völlig kindisch", *Der Spiegel* 26/2004 p 112

FERGUSON, Niall, "Europe gets my vote", *The Guardian* URL http://election.guardian.co.uk/eu/comment/0,9236,1249455,00.html, on Web June 2004

FRIED, Nico, "'In der Geschichte geht es nicht zu wie im Gesangsverein'", *Süddeutsche Zeitung* 25 June 2004 p 5

GRICE, Andrew, "Brown backs the PM: Blair will lead us into referendum in two years", *The Independent* 22 June 2004 p 4-5

GRICE, Andrew and WOOLF, Marie "Blair fires first shot in referendum fight", *The Independent* 21 June 2004 p 22

KAUFMANN, Bruno, "Five Spanish Lessons for Europe", URL http://euobserver.com/?aid=18459&sid=7, on Web 21 February 2005

KIRK, Lisbeth, "Finland set adopt European Constitution", URL http://euobserver.com/?aid=16701&sid=18, on Web July 2004

KIRK, Lisbeth, "Finnish Prime Minister rules out EU Constitution referendum", URL http://www.euobserver.com/?sid=9&aid=17088, on Web August 2004

LEICHT, Robert, "Mission Impossible: Verfassung für Europa", *Die Zeit* URL http://zeus.zeit.de/text/archiv/2002/10/200210_verfassgsmodelle.xml, on Web June 2004

LESSER, Gabriele, "'Morgen ist auch noch ein Tag'", *Kölner Stadt-Anzeiger* 15 December 2004 p 2

MAHONY, Honor, "Constitution negotiations reach fever pitch", URL http://euobserver.com/?aid=15603&sid=9, on Web July 2004

MAHONY, Honor, "Constitution set to be signed end of October", URL http://euobserver.com/?aid=16859&sid=18, on Web July 2004

MAHONY, Honor, "Countdown to final Constitution talks begins", URL http://euobserver.com/?aid=16607&sid=9, on Web July 2004

MAHONY, Honor, "Date set for Constitution signing", URL http://euobserver.com/?aid=16801&sid=18, on Web July 2004

MAHONY, Honor, "Debate on referendum heats up in Germany", URL http://euobserver.com/?aid=16936&sid=18, on Web July 2004

MAHONY, Honor, "France to have referendum on the Constitution", URL http://euobserver.com/?aid=16899&sid=9, on Web July 2004

MAHONY, Honor, "Germany and Austria moot Europe-wide constitution referendum", URL http://euobserver.com/?aid=15320&sid=9, on Web July 2004

MAHONY, Honor, "Germany and France produce plan B for treaty ratification", URL http://euobserver.com/?aid=16005&sid=9, on Web July 2004

MAHONY, Honor, "Movement on voting issue in Constitution", URL http://euobserver.com/?aid=16223&sid=9, on Web July 2004

MAHONY, Honor, "Ireland ups the pressure on Constitution talks", URL http://euobserver.com/?aid=15110&sid=9, on Web July 2004

MAHONY, Honor, "Poles may call referendum on Constitution", URL http://euobserver.com/?aid=15376&sid=9, on Web July 2004

MAHONY, Honor, "Schröder wants Constitution ratification in 2004", URL http://euobserver.com/?aid=16926&sid=9, on Web July 2004

McSMITH, Andy, "Leaders under fire from right – and Pope", *The Independent on Sunday* 20 June 2004 p 20

McSMITH, Andy, "Muddled message delivered by 'pro-Europe' premier", *The Independent on Sunday* 20 June 2004 p 20

MORRIS, Nigel, "Britain may not stay in EU if vote on constitution is lost, says Hewitt", *The Independent* 24 June 2004 p 23

NASH, Elizabeth, "Spain says 'yes' to constitution but barely two in five turn out to vote", http://news.independent.co.uk/europe/story.jsp?story=613150, on Web 21 February 2005

NONNENMACHER, Peter, "Blair hat 'Schlacht um Europa' eröffnet", *Kölner Stadt-Anzeiger* 21 April 2004 p 5

RENTOUL, John, "His policy on Europe is a failure. But can you really blame the man ?" (2004), *The Independent* 22 June 2004 p 24

REYNOLDS, Paul, "Constitution a hard-won compromise", *BBC News* URL http://news.bbc.co.uk/1/hi/world/europe/3820557.stm, on Web June 2004

RICHARDS, Steve, "Tony Blair has both the arguments and the passion to win this referendum" (2004), *The Independent* 22 June 2004 p 31

ROSS, Jan, "Huch, das Volk soll abstimmen", *Die Zeit* URL http://zeus.zeit.de/text/2004/19/Europa_2fVolk, on Web June 2004

ROXBURGH, Angus, "Referendum danger for EU", *BBC News* URL http://news.bbc.co.uk/1/hi/world/europe/3115674.stm, on Web June 2004

SCHULZE, Ralph, "Eindeutiges Ja zur EU-Verfassung", *Kölner Stadt-Anzeiger*, 21 February 2005

SCHULZE, Ralph, "Spanischer Test für EU-Verfassung", *Kölner Stadt-Anzeiger* 18 February 2005

SHARROCK, David, "Spain says 'si' to EU constitution", URL http://www.timesonline.co.uk/printFriendly/0,,1-13090-1493607,00.html, on Web 21 February 2005

SPITERI, Sharon, "Spain: referendum on Constitution as soon as possible", URL http://euobserver.com/?aid=16718&sid=9, on Web July 2004

QUENETT, Sibylle, "In Deutschland gibt es keinen Volksentscheid" (2004), *Kölner Stadt-Anzeiger* 21 April 2004 p 5

ULRICH, Stefan, "Europa in müder Verfassung", URL http://www.sueddeutsche.de/ausland/artikel/226/48178/print.html, on Web 22 February 2005

(viii) No author named

BBC NEWS, "Press relief over EU deal", URL http://news.bbc.co.uk/1/hi/world/europe/3821533.stm, on Web July 2004

COMMENT & ANALYSIS, "With referendum ahead, Blair must start saying Yes", *The Independent* 20 June 2004 p 24

DER SPIEGEL, "Politiker aller Fraktionen plädieren für Vertragswerk", URL http://www.spiegel.de/politik/ deutschland/0,1518,343454,00.html, on Web 24 February 2005

DER SPIEGEL, "Spanien stimmt für EU-Verfassung", URL http://www.spiegel.de/politik/ausland/0,1518,342798,00.html, on Web 20 February 2005

EDITORIAL COMMENTS, "The failure to reach an agreement on the EU Constitution – Hard Questions" (2004), *41 Common Market Law Review (C.M.L.Rev.)* 1-4

EDITORIAL COMMENTS, "The sixteen articles: On the way to a European Constitution" (2003), *40 Common Market Law Review (C.M.L.Rev.)* 267-277

EDITORIAL & OPINION, "There can be no delay in confronting the ingrained myths about Europe", *The Independent* 21 June 2004 p 24

EDITORIAL & OPINION, "After seven long years, the Prime Minister comes out fighting for the European cause", *The Independent* 22 June 2004 p 30

EL PAÍS, "Victoria aplastante del 'sí' en el referédum del Tratado Europeo", URL http://www.elpais.es/comunes/2005/ constitucion_europea/index.html, on Web February 2005

EURACTIV.COM, "Constitutional Treaty – key elements", URL http://www.euractiv.com/cgi-bin/cgint.exe?204&OIDN=20007 96&-home= home, on Web July 2004

EURACTIV.COM, "Referenda on EU Constitution –let the people vote ?", URL http://www.euractiv.com/cgi-bin/cgint.exe/ 1900561-478?714&1015=3&101 4=constref, on Web June 2004

EUROBAROMETER, "2004 Spring – Comparative Highlight Report: Table 10. National vs. European identity", EB 61 – CC-EB 2004.1, URL http://europa.eu.int/comm/public_opinion/archives/cceb/2004/cceb_2004.1_highlights.pdf, on Web July 2004

EUROPEAN-REFERENDUM.ORG, "Referendum on the EU-Constitution", URL http://european-referendum.org/about/ media.html, on Web July 2004

FUTURUM, "Ratification of the European Constitution", URL http://europa.eu.int/futurum/referendum_en.htm, on Web June 2004

KÖLNER STADT-ANZEIGER "Das Volk als Souverän oder 'Vox populi – vox Rindvieh'", *Kölner Stadt-Anzeiger* 29 July 2004, p 24

LEADING ARTICLE, "A flawed document", URL http://www.thetimes.co.uk, on Web June 2004

SÜDDEUTSCHE ZEITUNG, "Spanien sagt Ja zur EU-Verfassung", URL http://www.sueddeutsche.de/ausland/artikel/137/48089/ print.html, on Web 20 February 2005

THE DAILY MAIL, "EU Constitution – the main points", 19 June 2004 *The Daily Mail*, http://www.dailymail.co.uk/ pages/live/articles/news/news.html?in_article_id=307249&in_pa ge_id=1770, on Web August 2004

THE ECONOMIST, "A difficult birth", *376 The Economist* 26 June 2004, pp 41-42

THE ECONOMIST, "What it all means", *376 The Economist* 26 June 2004, p 42

Europa 2000
Studien zur interdisziplinären
Deutschland- und Europaforschung
hrsg. von der Arbeitsstelle für
Interdisziplinäre Deutschland- und
Europaforschung am Institut für
Politikwissenschaft
der Westfälischen Wilhelms-Universität
Münster

Dietmar Scholz
Abenteuer Europa
Geschichte und Identität Europas – Aufgaben und Probleme der Europäischen Union
Bd. 18, 1999, 168 S., 12,90 €, br.,
ISBN 3-8258-4124-3

Karl Hahn; Kerstin Kellermann;
Karsten Roesler (Hg.)
Fragen an Deutschlands Zukunft und seine Stellung in Europa
Deutschlands Zukunft ist fragwürdig: Eine klare und kritische Einschätzung zur vielzitierten "Lage der Nation" und ihrer Zukunftsfähigkeit in Europa verlangt nicht nur die Funktionstüchtigkeit des politischen Systems in den Blick zu nehmen. Konsequent ist darüber hinaus nach der substantiellen demokratischen Wirklichkeit der Republik, der politischen Kultur und des öffentlichen Lebens in Deutschland zu fragen. Dies gilt vor allem hinsichtlich der notwendigen Voraussetzungen, Optionen einer Bürgergesellschaft in die Tat umzusetzen. Dabei scheuen sich die AutorInnen der interdisziplinären Beiträge nicht, Tabuthemen anzusprechen und offene Fragen auch als solche zu behandeln.
Bd. 19, 2001, 240 S., 25,90 €, br.,
ISBN 3-8258-4919-8

Viktor Major
Kaliningrad/Königsberg: Auf dem schweren Weg zurück nach Europa
Bestandsaufnahme und Zukunftsvisionen aus einer europäischen Krisenregion
Die russische Exklave Kaliningrad, die – zumindest aus westlicher Perzeption – über Jahrzehnte hinweg nahezu in Vergessenheit geriet, läßt sich angesichts der dramatischen politischen Veränderungen in den Staaten Ostmitteleuropas kaum länger an den Rand der öffentlichen Wahrnehmung drängen. Welche Alternativen sind für die zukünftige Entwicklung der Region vor allem auch im Rahmen der Osterweiterung der EU denkbar? Um das Entwicklungspotential mit der notwendigen Sachkenntnis zu analysieren und in seiner Tragfähigkeit einzuschätzen, ist zunächst eine profunde Deskription der gegenwärtigen Lage insbesondere in ihren vielfältigen Krisenerscheinungen und Spannungsfeldern unverzichtbar. Das vorliegende Buch stellt hierzu einen richtungsweisenden Beitrag dar.
Bd. 20, 2001, 160 S., 15,90 €, br.,
ISBN 3-8258-5721-2

Natalia Daniliouk; Karsten Roesler;
Philipp Hermeier (Hg.)
Russland – Deutschland – Europa
Angesichts der Unterzeichnung der Beitrittsverträge zur Europäischen Union durch die zehn ost- und mittelosteuropäischen Regierungschefs Mitte April 2003 sprach Bundeskanzler Gerhard Schröder von der „Aufhebung der europäischen Teilung in einen Osten und einen Westen". Doch insbesondere im Kontext des Irak-Krieges wurden erhebliche Risse im Fundament des ‚Gemeinsamen europäischen Hauses' offenbar. Wie steht es also mit der Einheit Europas, mit dem Verhältnis zwischen Ost und West? Welche Rolle sollte Europa im transatlantischen Kräftespiel einnehmen – und welcher Stellenwert ist dabei vor allem den deutsch-russischen Beziehungen beizumessen? Diese hochaktuellen Fragen werden in diesem interdisziplinären Tagungsband, herausgegeben zu Ehren des Münsteraner Politikwissenschaftlers Prof. em. Dr. Karl Hahn, in Fachbeiträgen in- und ausländischer Wissenschaftler aus den unterschiedlichsten Blickwinkeln betrachtet und analysiert.
Bd. 21, 2004, 304 S., 24,90 €, br.,
ISBN 3-8258-7143-6

LIT Verlag Münster – Berlin – Hamburg – London – Wien
Grevener Str./Fresnostr. 2 48159 Münster
Tel.: 0251 – 62 03 22 – Fax: 0251 – 23 19 72
e-Mail: vertrieb@lit-verlag.de – http://www.lit-verlag.de